Into the Sun

Also by Colin B. Douglas:

First Light, First Water
Glyphs
Division by Zero
Six Poems by Joseph Smith

INTO THE SUN

Poems Revised, Rearranged, and New

COLIN B. DOUGLAS

WAKING LION PRESS

Cover: *Five Dancing Angels,* by Giovanni di Paolo, oil and gold on panel, about 1436.

Copyright © 2019 by Colin B. Douglas. All rights reserved.
Printed in the United States of America.

ISBN 978-1-4341-0419-9

The views expressed in this book are the responsibility of the author and do not necessarily represent the position of the publisher. The reader alone is responsible for the use of any ideas or information provided by this book.

Parts of this book are works of fiction. The characters, places, and incidents in them are the products of the author's imagination or are represented fictitiously. Any resemblance of characters or events to actual persons or events is coincidental.

Published by Waking Lion Press, an imprint of The Editorium

Waking Lion Press™, the Waking Lion Press logo, and The Editorium™ are trademarks of The Editorium, LLC

The Editorium, LLC
West Jordan City, UT 84081-6132
wakinglionpress.com
wakinglion@editorium.com

Contents

Preface	1
Creation myth	2
Another creation myth	3
Doctrine and Covenants	4
I am told of a certain tree	5
I sought you, Adonai	6
Adonai, forsake me not	7
Adonai, I have sinned	8
Prayer	9
Like a deer he comes to me	10
Adonai, cover me with your robe	11
The earth upon her wings moves not so quietly	12
A separate peace	13
The grasses sing and the trees shout	14
Let the stone whisper to the flower	15
A daughter of Sarah is my beloved	16

My beloved shall be mine beyond death	17
Wedding songs	18
More wedding songs	20
Deer come down from the hills	22
Deer have passed here	23
A cup of water in the High Uintas	24
Haiku	25
On Lake Mountain	26
Coordinates	27
Outside the longhouse	28
Peel back a bit of skin and see	29
Luminous books	30
Last night's equations	31
Girl on a platform	32
Girl on bridge beckons	33
Tangle of roads, houses, seas	34
I don't know why the moon is white	35

MIRROR HALF HIDDEN BY FALLEN LEAVES	36
A WALK IN THE WOODS	37
THE VISION OF ALL BECOMES	38
NO MEMORY	39
A LONG HALLWAY	40
A GIRL FLOATS ON A RIVER OF LIGHT	41
THERE IS NO INTEREST IN PASCAL	42
A MAN REMEMBERS	43
ADVENTURES OF A YOUNG MAN	44
A TALE OF DETECTION	53
A NEW JOB	59
WAYSTATION	61
THERE ARE SEVERAL REASONS WHY THIS WON'T WORK	63
YELLOW SNAKES	64
ON A THURSDAY	66
BANNERS OF PAST LIVES	68
HOMECOMING	70

A DOOR STANDS OPEN, BEYOND IT THE SUN	72
TRAIL DESCENDS AND NARROWS	74
A SPHERE GROWS INSIDE MY BREAST	75
LOOKING DOWN A NARROW VALLEY	76
PREGNANT MOVING VANS JOSTLE TOGETHER ON THE HIGHWAY	78
THE DOVES OF MINIMAL EFFICIENCY	79
THE APEX OF AN ISOSCELES TRIANGLE	80
FISHHOOKS TIED TO SILKEN FILAMENTS	81
WALKING IN THE SHADOW OF THE SUN'S MEMORY	82
THE DELICATE MUSIC OF THE SPHERES	83
THE INDECISION OF A LARK'S TONGUE	84
DAWN BREAKS CRIMSON FROM THE MUSIC BOX	85
A DREAM WRAPPED IN RAIN WRAPPED IN A DREAM	86
THE DAY ARRIVES LATE	87
THE TUMESCENT ORCHID THAT LIES IGNORED ON THE ALTAR	88
THE PIANO KEYS MELT SLOWLY IN THE AFTERNOON SUN	89
A THREAD OF LIGHT FLOATS	90

THOUGH I FEARED WE MIGHT FIND HAPPINESS TOGETHER	91
I KEEP YOUR KISSES IN A BOX	92
I HIDE IN THE DEEP GRASS OF MY HEART	93
THE TWISTED ROPE OF DAY	94
SUCH HAPPINESS IS RARE	95
AS AN AUTOMOBILE SOARS OFF A CLIFF'S EDGE	96
A BOOK OF LAMENTATIONS	97
LOOKING FOR THE CAPTAIN	103
LET THERE BE LIGHT	105
LINGERING OVER A PAGE OF GENESIS	107
PEEL THE WALLS AWAY FROM THE BRAIN	108
BLUE HAND YELLOW HAND	109
THE MOON SWOLLEN IN LATE PREGNANCY	110
PASSING THROUGH THE ASPEN GROVE BEATING HAND DRUMS	111
A NEARLY FULL MOON RISING BEHIND THE MOUNTAINS	112
CUT A SLIT ON THE SURFACE OF THE LAKE	113
ON THESE TWO PRONGS OF A DEER'S ANTLER	115

WHITE MASK PEOPLE AND YELLOW MASK PEOPLE	116
A WOMAN STANDS BEFORE AN OPEN WINDOW	117
BEYOND THE FURTHEST RIDGE	118
A GIANTESS PEELS BACK THE SKIN OF THE EARTH	119
AT THE END OF THE EVENING	120
THE UNDONE HAIR OF SATISFIED DESIRE	121
SEVEN TRAILS	122
QUARTET	123
WALL ATTEMPTS TO COVER ITS BREASTS	131
ARS POETICA	132
PORTRAIT OF THE ARTIST AS A YOUNG MAN	136
"YOUR POEMS ARE QUERULOUS"	137
A PARABOLA SUPINE ON THE FLOOR	138
"HELP ME," YOU SAY	139
A GRAND PIANO ON A PIER	140
SIXTEEN SMALL STONES	141
SILENT MEDITATIONS ON TORN LINGERIE	142

YOUR EYES WIDE BEHIND MINE	143
BENEATH LITTERED STREETS PERSIST RUMORS OF ILL WILL	144
A BATTLE TANK LADEN WITH VIOLETS	145
AXELS ROLL AND CLANG DOWN A DESERT HIGHWAY	146
LET BOTH THY LEGS BE SPINNING TOPS	147
AGAINST BLACK A TORSO	148
SUSPENDED IN SPACE	149
TEXTBOOK SOLUTIONS ALWAYS LEAK	150
THIS ROSE UNFOLDING ITS PETALS	151
MELCHIZEDEK AND HIS BRIDE	152
A SPIRIT RISES FROM OUR BED	153
IS NOT BABYLON A GOLDEN CUP IN THE LORD'S HAND?	154
A RAINBOW STRAIGHTENS; IT IS A FLOWER STEM	155
DANEEL OLIVAW AND ANDRÉ BRETON ARE RAFTING TO TAHITI	156
YOU UNLOCK YOURSELF	157
PROVERBS	158
THE URIM OF A JEWELRY BOX WHISPERS ENDEARMENTS	159

Rain falls through the night	160
In the place where rain flies upward from the earth	161
Behind a waterfall an abandoned service station	162
The hour is nigh and the day soon at hand	164
The first time I saw rain through an Edward Hopper painting	165
The reason I stole shoes from the legs of an easel in the MOMA	166
This is no accident	167
And God called the light Day	168
Speaking of old books	169
The old woman who lives in deep woods	170
In the No Thing from which all things rise	171
The skin of a telephone pole	172
The table is set in the banquet hall	173
A flock of starlings collapsing suddenly to a period	174
Here is the secret exit from the theater of the mind	175
A man in orange coveralls and safety goggles	176

SITTING IN A CAMP CHAIR IN A PATCH OF ALDERS	177
THE LAKE'S NIPPLES QUIVER UNDER THE GAZE OF A RECEDING PARAGRAPH	178
AT THE HORIZON LINE OF MY WOMAN'S SHOULDER	179
A CONTINGENT OF UNDEFINED PAIN STAGES AN INCIDENT ON THE BORDER	180
I CANNOT FIND YOUR KISSES ON THIS MAP	181
FLEEING THE SCENE	182
A SALAL LEAF GROWS FROM MY PALM	183
I RECEIVE A LETTER FROM A WOMAN PROMISING LOVE AT AN UNSPECIFIED DATE	185
YOUR BREASTS ARE BIRD'S EGGS	186
THE WOMAN IN THE STREET HUDDLES UNDER HER WINGS	187
A PERIOD WORKING ITS WAY DOWN THE TUBE OF A THERMOMETER	188
"YE WERE ALSO—IN THE BEGINNING"	189
ALWAYS THE FIRST TIME?	190
SMALL SNAKE COILED	191
AN EYE IN EACH FINGERTIP	192

Walking in a garden we see in the distance clocks	193
Arrican France, for a time	194
Driving a blue convertible on a country road	195
The prairie grass in my heart	196
In the grass-infested cylinders of a Model T engine	197
Remorse is a decaying house on the outskirts of town	198
I attach great importance to life	199
Curl of a hand	201
Open the abdomen of the sun	202
The white deer that walks in the hallway	205
A breaker curling over onto the shore	206
I do not know why deer wade up to their knees in blood of doubt	207
As I round a bend in a canoe a doe is swimming	208
We should talk, *bon Gérard*	209
Tactical maneuver	210
I find you at the box end	212
The old woman who carries a basket on her back	213

DO YOU THINK GOD WANTS TO WITHDRAW HIS AD?	214
GOD IS THAT FAT WOMAN IN THE APRON	215
AS WE SIT TOGETHER IN THE LIVING ROOM OF THE OLD HOUSE	216
Existenz	217
THE SEWING MACHINE NEEDLE OF TRUTH FLOATS FREE	218
SNOWFLAKES DISTANCE THEMSELVES FROM THE PRESIDENT	219
SQUANTO STEPS ON A DRY TWIG	220
AFTER THE NEXT WAR	221
STARING DOWN A FISH	223
A SONG FOR THE LADY	224
COMPOSITION IN TWO MOVEMENTS	237
THE POSTING	248
POEM KIT; SOME ASSEMBLY REQUIRED	250
SNOWFLAKES FLOAT OUT FROM THE CENTER POINT	251
THE DOORKNOB OF THE LOGOS	252
A MIST OF EQUATIONS	253
ELK THAT WRAPS ITS ANTLERS IN SKEINS OF YELLOW SILK	258

In Quito, Ecuador	259
The Being that contains all things	260
The smell of a clean cotton dress	261
Lactation of a white marble statue	262
And we walk among the alders	263
The sad song of derangement	264
The Watchers on the hills wring their hands in anguish	265
The deer serene	267
Note to a young Mormon poet	268
A boy sits at a table	269
Exchanging white stones engraved with our names	270
Author's note	271
Biographical note	273
Acknowledgments	274

Preface

Somewhere among words
An opening
Search among words
As between a beloved's legs
Somewhere an opening
Somewhere light
Somewhere water
First Light
First Water

Creation myth

That which says "I AM"—
That which is Spirit,
Even the Spirit of truth—
Knows itself first
Through the eyes of
Eternal Mother/Eternal Father
As they look each upon the other,
And in their mutual love and desire is
Beginning.

Another creation myth

*A revision of the King Follett Discourse,
with apologies to Joseph Smith and a nod to Eliza Snow*

Eternal Man and Eternal Woman (they are the Gods)
find themselves in the midst of intelligences and glory.
Because they are greater,
the Gods see proper
to beget the lesser intelligences as their spirit children
and to let Eternal Man institute laws
whereby they can have a privilege
to advance like themselves
and be exalted with them,
so that the lesser intelligences might have one glory upon another
in all that knowledge, power, and glory.
So they take in hand to save the world of intelligences.
Eternal Man speaks to Eternal Woman,
"Let it be so,"
and she answers,
"That is my desire, also;
let it be so";
and they couple,
and she gives birth to the intelligences as their spirit children;
and thus the Gods are
Eternal Father and Eternal Mother.

Doctrine and Covenants

*Thy dominion shall be an everlasting dominion,
and without compulsory means it shall flow unto thee
forever and ever.*

—D&C 121:46

Words: *matter, element, spirit, intelligence,
light, glory, agency, male, female, God, man.*
And behind the words?
Say *I* and there is *you;*
Say *light* and there is *darkness;*
Yes and there is *no.*
It comes to this:
Lover receiving lover,
Flow of seed,
Flow of light, galaxies, worlds, plants, beasts, man and woman,
Then children, tribes, cities, wars and rumors of wars,
The cross, the empty tomb, a sea of glass;
But it comes to this:
My love, I touch your face,
Your kiss is tender.
Let us lie down in the grass.

I am told of a certain tree

I am told of a certain tree,
And a certain well:
That the fruit of the tree
And the water from the well
Are unspeakably sweet;
And I have tasted fruit no man could name,
And water whose source no man could tell,
And having tasted
I know of greater folly
Than to seek that tree
And that well.

I sought you, Adonai

Ye shall seek me, and find me.

—Jeremiah 29:13

I sought you, Adonai, and I found you.
I sought you among the firs and the alders,
Among the stars of clear skies.
I found you not there.
I sought you on hilltops,
I sought you in clear streams,
In the gold and red of trout,
And I found you not there.
But in the clouded and starless night
When I sought you with tears,
When I knelt in ashes,
I found you; your finger touched me.
And now, among the firs and the alders,
Among stars and on hilltops,
In clear streams
And in the gold and red of trout,
I find you, Adonai,
I find you.

Adonai, forsake me not

The Lord knoweth how to deliver the godly out of temptations.

—2 Peter 2:9

Adonai, forsake me not,
Turn not away.
Sin like a girl comes whispering,
Like a girl with light fingers,
Whispering softly.

Adonai, I have sinned

Touch these stones, O Lord, with thy finger.

—Ether 3:4

Adonai, I have sinned;
I have sinned grievously against you.
My legs are water, my bowels burn;
My bowels are hot stone.
Silence encloses me like iron walls;
I cannot hear your voice.
I have sinned against you,
And your voice is shut out.
As you touched the small stones,
Reach forth to touch me;
Make me clean as burning stone.
I have loved you in time past;
I have embraced your fire.
Embrace me now in my uncleanness.

Prayer

Remember not the sins of my youth.

—*Psalm 25:7*

Father, my sins are not hidden from you;
upon my bed I remember them.
Before my shut eyes they dance
and watch me with solemn mockery.
I would forget them;
will you not remove them?
Let there be a garden of tulips before me,
washed by spring rain;
walk in it with me.
As a raindrop on a tulip petal,
so would I be before you.

Like a deer he comes to me

Take, eat: this is my body.

—Mark 14:22

Like a deer he comes to me,
Parting the ferns,
Like a deer with bright antlers.
I chase him across meadows,
Beside streams I pursue him,
And he does not weary;
But in the thicket he surprises me,
He lets my arrow pierce him.
He gives me of his flesh at evening,
And in the bright morning
Like a deer he comes to me.

Adonai, cover me with your robe

That the Lord shall give thee rest

—2 Nephi 24:3

Adonai, cover me with your robe;
Let me rest against you.
I have traveled in far places;
Where you have sent me, I have gone.
Among serpents I have laid my bed;
I have risen to go among wolves.
I have walked in dry places
Where the rocks held no water;
I have crossed high mountains
Where frost was my covering.
I have gone unshod;
My feet have bled.
I am weary;
I have found no rest.
Let me rest against you;
Shelter me with your robe.

The earth upon her wings moves not so quietly

The earth rolls upon her wings

—D&C 88:45

The earth upon her wings moves not so quietly
As He walks in corridors of light.
Morning mists, the bloom of flowers,
Air still on meadows—
More quietly than these He goes.

A SEPARATE PEACE

Wo, wo is me, the mother of men.

—Moses 7:48

Earth the mother of men:
Then is not Sun,
By whose seed of light Earth conceives,
The father of men?
And Moon is sister,
And every creature brother or sister.
I greet you,
My family,
My tribe:
Father Sun,
Mother Earth,
Sister Moon,
Brother and Sister Raven,
Brother and Sister Coyote.
All creatures,
My brothers and sisters,
I weep with you,
And in the Creator
With you I hope.
Let there be peace between us.

The grasses sing and the trees shout

Behold, and lo, the Bridegroom cometh.

—D&C 88:92

The grasses sing and the trees shout
As Shaddai descends to receive his bride.
The stones laugh and the rivers leap;
As he kisses her mouth, the clouds rain wine.
In the meadows of Eden he lies with her,
And the issue of her womb is heavenly lights.

Let the stone whisper to the flower

Behold, and lo, the Bridegroom cometh

—D&C 88:92

Let the stone whisper to the flower,
The flower to the sun,
And the sun to the stars of heaven,
That Jehovah is come for his bride;
She bends her knee graciously to him.
The sun hides its face,
And all silvering clouds, all shimmering snow
Are darkness to the light of her raiment.
He calls her Zion;
He lifts her by the hand.
The stone whispers to the flower
And the flower to the sun
That his kiss is tender.
The table is set; the wine is served;
And the stars break forth in song.

A Daughter of Sarah Is My Beloved

If a man marry a wife by the new and everlasting covenant

—D&C 132:19

A daughter of Sarah is my beloved,
A priestess in Abraham's house.
Her knee is bent to the Lord;
She dwells within the circle of his law.
For virtue she is clean as rain,
As streams that descend high slopes.
Her smile is as sunlight on meadows,
Her speech a sparrow's flight for gentleness.
Her counsel is heard in the congregation;
To the ears of the wise she speaks wisdom.
She gives bread to those who have not asked;
The afflicted receive comfort at her hand.
Her love she has not withheld from me;
She has given me all delights.
Sons and daughters she has given me;
Our generations will fill the heavens.
Our covenant will stand forever;
Beyond death I shall know her embrace.
Though the earth melt at His coming,
I shall never be parted from her.

My beloved shall be mine beyond death

If a man marry a wife by the new and everlasting covenant

—*D&C 132:19*

My beloved shall be mine beyond death,
For by His sure nails we are joined.
Though our bones go down to darkness,
I shall never be parted from her.
With the just we await the dawn;
In the morning we shall rise with the sun.
Our children will gather about us;
On Mount Zion we shall stand together.
In the fields of a new earth I shall embrace her;
In the gardens of a new Eden she will receive me.
Our generations will fill the heavens,
And worlds without end will honor her.

Wedding songs

If a man marry a wife by the new and everlasting covenant

—*D&C 132:19*

1

On the first morning of our marriage,
You gave me raspberries in a white bowl.
Later we stood barefoot on sand
And let white sea foam wash about our ankles.

2

We lay down among flowers,
The grass sweet and wet,
Your dress wet.
Horses came near under blue sky,
Treading down the sweet grass,
And your dress was yellow among the flowers.

3

The whiteness of foam,
The smell of morning rain;
And as we walked on the sand,
My fingertips touched your sleeve.

4

I come with gifts of milk and wine,
Silver shoes, and a bough of cherries,
And enter your garden of roses.

5

Your hand through the parted veil,
And later, the forked flame of your thighs.
Sarai's limbs in Abram's tent
Could not have burned more bright.

More wedding songs

Who is she that looketh forth as the morning, fair as the sun, clear as the moon, terrible as an army with banners?

—*Song of Solomon 6:10*

1

Flute songs float up from your hair,
A tulip is one eye and a daffodil the other,
Clouds of butterflies are the skin of your belly,
Meadows of fresh grass are your thighs,
Honeybees make a hive of your bowels,
A rising sun in clear sky tips each of your fingers,
A galaxy revolves in black space on each of your palms,
White-water rivers cascade from beneath your toenails,
Armies with bright banners gallop across a plain
Beyond the gateway of your sex.

2

I fall into you as into a dream of a house.
The front doors open outward wide.
I tumble through
To roll into an ocean of flowers vermillion

3

My hands grasp your ribcage,
Stars are your nipples.

4

Your ribcage holds the sun,
Light streams between my fingers.

5

In the orchard
Swollen fruit,
Wet grass tangled,
Sunlight refracted in raindrops
Shining in the veins.

6

My hands cupped about your breasts,
A thumb over each nipple.
Your eyes open to meet mine.

Deer come down from the hills

Deer come down from the hills,
Down the ravines,
Dry creek beds;
Grass dry,
Wind cold.
The high hills are colder,
Dusted by snow.
Your eyes are brown as a deer's.

Deer have passed here

Deer have passed here,
A doe, a fawn,
Maybe a buck—
Those tracks are bigger.
They come down in moonlight
To browse on green corn.
Silent as moonlight
They pass.

A cup of water in the High Uintas

Snow
Granite
Spruce and quakies
Meadow
Streams
Join to become
The Duchesne
Green
Colorado
Gulf of California
Pacific
And beyond—
Here I drink
Of the Black Sea
And of rain on the Kirgiz Steppe

Haiku

Airplane turning above mountain—
Brightness
Of steel and snow

Cirrus on blue sky—
Snow powder
Blown up from the ridge

From glacial pool
Trout
Stares back

Low tide
Mudflat
White of empty clam shells

On Lake Mountain

Maples red and orange,
Snow on distant ridge,
Breeze coming somewhere off ice,
Badger's white skull under juniper—
My dog runs a trail
On Lake Mountain in October.

Coordinates

Feet on rock
Sun before
Moon behind
Four ravens above

Outside the Longhouse

Early light through low clouds,
Beach at low tide,
Canoes drawn up,
Smell of alder smoke,
My woman still wrapped in bear robe.
Last night I dreamed Raven stole our fire.

Peel back a bit of skin and see

Peel back a bit of skin and see
The sun blazing over stone and sand
And rivulets of light
Trickling through crevices of fear.

Luminous books

Luminous books,
A pool of fish flaming,
Snow rising through grass.
What is this book that speaks
Of snow and fish and grass?

Last night's equations

Last night's equations are inscribed on the eyes of morning.
A woman holds in her teeth the moon
As delicately as Urim balanced on the tip of a salmon's fin.
The moon slips from her teeth,
The eyes of morning take its place.
The equations float,
White feathers back into the night.

Girl on a platform

Girl on a platform,
Hair of pearls floating on the wind,
Turns slowly counterclockwise,
Raises her right arm toward the sky,
Hair of pearls floating,
Speaks one unheard syllable,
Inscribes a question on the wind.

Girl on bridge beckons

Girl on bridge beckons
Girl in dress of broken glass
Girl with teeth of early snow
Girl whose legs are pillars on a distant hill
Girl with hair of ivy where small birds nest
Girl whose eyes are open doorways
Girl who knows what is written behind the mirror

Tangle of roads, houses, seas

Tangle of roads, houses, seas
Tangle of hallways and doors and glass
Of seas and rocks and shoals and shores
A face beyond the tangled highways of the sun

I don't know why the moon is white

For Charles Cros

I don't know why the moon is white
I don't know where the butterflies sleep
I don't know why a man leans a ladder against a white wall
Or why the wall curves gently away

Mirror half hidden by fallen leaves

Mirror half hidden by fallen leaves,
White hand extended through the glass—
Deer pass through the clearing one by one
And do not leave a scrap of paper to blow
Across the grass in a hot wind
Beneath a white sun obscured by antlers.
Eyes unblinking in the glare,
We watch from behind a corner of a distant building
And wait to fall into the mirror.

A WALK IN THE WOODS

A walk in the woods
Leaves brown and golden
Golden towers rising above the trees
Girls on the lake shore
Naked, watchful,
Eyes of red stop lights
Swinging in the wind on a single cable
Storm rising in the east
Rain washing the towers
Plastic blowing in the wind
Wraps about the girls

The vision of all becomes

The vision of all becomes
As a face peering through leaves,
Expressionless,
Wordless,
A tangle of branches and leaves,
Behind them a mirror set against a tree trunk
And in the mirror a face,
The trees veiled in snow.
Ecstatic beneath the sun.

No memory

No memory
No feet
No eyes
No light
No darkness
No pendants flapping in the breeze
No yellow pendants
No blue pendants
No red pendants
No face looking up from beneath the surface of the water
No lovers entwined among the ferns
No book lying open beneath the sun
No voice

A long hallway

A long hallway
Old wallpaper
Old carpet
Musty smell
Bare dim light bulbs hanging by cords from the ceiling
Yellowed white-painted doors
Many doors both sides of the hallway
The hallway not straight
It curves gradually to the right
The line of sight cut off in the distance
Just before the lines converge
Whether the hallway makes a circle
That remains unanswered
But open a door and then another
Behind one a lilac grove
Behind another an empty room
Behind another a boulevard by the sea

A girl floats on a river of light

A girl floats on a river of light
Blue pelican love
And the boats drawn up on the beach
Where a girl rests against the rocks
Is this how it begins?
A mist rises from the river with an agate in its teeth
Bits of rags, red and yellow
Long strips of rags wrapped about a pole
A mouth wide open
Gleaming teeth
Waves swell and crash green and white
A woman in white floats among the trees
Rain falls steadily through the night
Ten minutes from the ocean
A difficult decision
The wings of a gull curve against a clear sky
A difficult decision

There is no interest in Pascal

There is no interest in Pascal,
But sparrows flock to the bust of Zeno.
The refugees scattered across the plain fear the smoke
   of burning lies,
But their fear is containable
So long as the mothers continue their vigil behind the mountains.
Tomorrow—we wait for tomorrow—
Maybe tomorrow the bust of Pascal will join the vigil.

A man remembers

A man remembers a house in a small town, in a country of firs and much rain. He awakes one night to the sound of rain on the roof, and unable to return to sleep he rises from his bed and goes to the back door to watch the rain fall. In a puddle near the door a pale plastic doll lies naked, face up. He is alone in this house, there are no children, and so he wonders how the doll has come to be there. There was a woman in this house the night before. He stood with her in the kitchen, kissing her mouth, his right hand lifting the hem of her dress. The doll is more pink than the skin of that woman. Near the house is an apple orchard, old and neglected, the trees overgrown, apples rotting on the ground. He likes the smell of the rotting apples in the fall. Beyond the orchard stand large old fir trees, and among the trees a house, white, two-storied. There are children there, but there is no reason why any of them should have been in his back yard, leaving a naked doll on the ground.

Adventures of a young man

He awakes in the dark in the earliest hours of the third day in a cheap hotel room to see standing at the foot of his bed the faint image of a young woman in a blue hooded cloak. She says, "Come, follow me; it is time." She turns and walks toward the door, and he rises, already dressed, and follows her out the door, leaving the door open and nothing behind him.

He follows her down the hallway, a narrow passage with yellow walls and a thin carpet of uncertain gray to brown, lighted at each end by a bare bulb hanging by a strand of electrical cord. Standing at one doorway with a hand on the knob is a man in red, at another a man in yellow, at a third a man in white; none of them looking at him as he passes, just staring at the floor as if trying to recall something.

He follows the woman down the stairway at the end of the hall, winding down three floors, into the lobby and past the desk clerk, who is asleep in his chair behind an iron grill, out onto the dark street, where she turns to the right and proceeds down the sidewalk.

The street is deserted, except for the three men: the man in red stands beneath a lamppost with his head and shoulders slightly bowed and his arms extended and hands apart as if holding a large package; the man in yellow stands at attention in the intersection ahead; the man in white stands inside the entryway of a shop that deals in curios from small and poor South American nations—blowguns; shrunken heads of Guaraní children; small refrigerators with missing doors; dresses worn by female impersonators who had performed in mediocre tourist hotels; a piece of damp, dark cloth with a slightly sour smell. (He saw all of this numerous times when he visited the store in his childhood; once with his father; several times, he thinks, with his mother and her sisters. He was in the store once at a time when it sold supplies and paraphernalia for spiritist rituals: table after table loaded with dusty tangles of herbs and grasses, candles, bottles of powdered viscera of bats and coral snakes, complete human skins stripped in the twinkling of an eye from unsuspecting office workers as they waited at bus stops and elevators, Haitian cigarettes in tin boxes, a profusion of small baskets and boxes woven of various natural fibers, small objects that he saw out of the corners of his eyes but was unable to bring into focus sufficiently long to identify them, and wild violets, jeweled with dew, pressing up everywhere through the endless piles of merchandise. Once, inside the shop, as he stood among the tables, he became vaguely anxious, fearful of being recognized as an enemy, and, looking about for a place to hide, he spied a large object of red glass and slipped behind it. As he looked through the thin and quite transparent glass, he gradually realized that this was a sculpture of a vulva, and he was standing within the curve of the concave side.)

Then the young man and his guide turn a corner and find themselves standing before an immense and ancient mansion, which he has never before noticed but which he recognizes has been there long before the city that surrounded it was conceived. It is many stories high, though he does not count. There are turrets and battlements and ledges, and windows of the deepest black; gargoyles and the Green Man everywhere; cornucopias spilling fruits and sheaves of grain; and carved along the faces of the ledges runes and glyphs and formulae and outlines of continents and scenes of love and hunting and battle. It is all in wine-red brick, in some places crumbling to dust that floats out onto the night air and falls slowly and silently toward the street: immensity and darkness looming against the stars, hovering doves, the possibility of a great forest within. The air bleeeds.

The mansion is surrounded by a stone wall surmounted by a spiked iron fence. They stand before a gate that curves high above them, and the woman says, "This is the house of which you have been told. You have choices, which are both few and many. Find the box containing the Urim and Thummim, and hope that you will remember their use. Take this ring, on which you see carved in bdellium the last letter of the alphabet of the angels. Now, go."

He climbs seventy steps to the door. Upon entering, he finds himself in a large foyer, the floor of which is cluttered with computer-like machines and instruments, which he recognizes as belonging to a French organization for the study of paranormal phenomena. To his right is another door into what appears to be a receptionist's room. Behind the receptionist's desk sits a young man, Somalian, he thinks, of urbane demeanor. He approaches the young man and stands before his desk. The man looks up and says: "Good morning, sir. I will be with you momentarily."

He punches two keys on his computer, adjusts a thin stack of papers, and returns his attention to his visitor.

"How may I help you, sir?"

Without speaking, the visitor holds the ring out to him. He takes it, examines it, and says, "I see. Well."

The receptionist hands back the ring and sits back in his chair and folds his hands on his desktop.

"We have been waiting for you for some time. Some of us were beginning to lose hope. Are you ready?"

"I suppose so. There was nowhere else to go."

"What instructions have you received?"

"'This is the house of which you have been told. You have choices, which are both few and many. Find the box containing the Urim and Thummim, and hope that you will remember their use. Take this ring, on which you see carved in bdellium the last letter of the alphabet of the angels. Now, go.' "

"That is not much to go on, is it?"

"No, I suppose not."

"Well, let me show you to the entrance. Whether you go on or not is, of course, up to you, though we do have our reasons for hoping you will."

The receptionist rises and takes the visitor back out to the foyer. At the rear of the foyer is a doorway the visitor did not notice when he first came in. The casing is plain and white, like that of a bedroom or a closet of an ordinary house. The door itself is missing, though the brass hinges are still in place. An unlighted staircase rises from just within the door. The steps are of bare wood, and worn.

"We haven't picked up any movement here for several months. That's all I can tell you."

The visitor stands in the doorway and looks up the stairs. They disappear into complete darkness about twenty steps up.

"All right," he says. "Thank you."

He climbs for a long time in the darkness. For a time he can see the bright rectangle of the door below when he looks back, but then it disappears. He supposes the stairway has turned slightly in one direction or the other, though he has not noticed which.

He comes to what seems to be a landing. Feeling about, he finds a door knob and turns it. The door opens inward into a hallway. He steps inside and shuts the door behind him.

He follows the hallway until it turns to the right, and he is standing inside a simple bedroom. A young woman—sandy-colored hair, a light gray sweatshirt, blue denim jeans—is making the bed. She flips out the white sheet, lets it settle, then works around the bed tucking the edges under the mattress. She makes hospital corners. She lays out the second sheet and tucks it under and makes hospital corners at the foot. She lays out a quilt and a spread, folds them back, puts pillows in place, and then tucks the bedding over them.

"The children are outside," she says. "I will call them for lunch in a few minutes."

She leaves the room, and he follows her.

The house is small. There is a small hallway from which two bedrooms and a bathroom open. The hallway opens into a living room, which is spacious for the size of the house. One door of the room opens directly outside, the other into the kitchen. This is a wooden frame house. The floors are wood, and the varnish has mostly worn off. The living room floor is partially covered by a large worn rug of the same material as the carpet in the hallway of the hotel.

The kitchen door stands open. It is a warm, sunny day. There is a screen door, and he stands at the kitchen door looking out through the screen. There is a yard with grass, a high wooden fence around the yard, big leafy trees outside the fence all around the yard. There are blue sky and white clouds, the sound of bees, the drone of an airplane, the sound of hammering.

The woman opens the refrigerator and takes out a glass bottle of milk and a package of baloney. She sets them on the counter. She takes a loaf of Wonder Bread in its white wrapper with red, blue, and yellow polka dots from a bread box and sets it on the counter. She makes a baloney sandwich and cuts it in half and puts the halves on separate plates. She makes a peanut butter and blackberry jam sandwich and cuts it and puts the halves on the plates. She puts a few potato chips on each plate. She pours milk into two glasses. She sets everything on the table, a Formica table with chromed legs and vinyl and chrome chairs.

He is standing on the grass near the fence when she calls the children. There is a smell of hot wood, the children frozen in the motions of going into the house, a bird frozen in the air just above the fence. A miniature of the glass vulva rests on a white embroidered cloth on the chest of drawers. A drawer slides open. As he reaches out to touch the denim over her knee, she lies back, a mound of yellow sweet-smelling flowers in the sun, as one wall of the bedroom is no longer there. Always, it has been like this. He walks away with a pang of disappointment to look for the second door, down the long hallway, past the man in red (where were the yellow and the white?), back into the stairwell, groping about in the darkness, finding the stairs upward, climbing again into the darkness.

The second door. Another hallway, along each side stalls from which, as he passes, men and women performing a variety of erotic acts, most of which he thinks he would not enjoy but some of which intrigue him, look up at him with hostile eyes. He comes to one stall that, unlike the others, is hidden by a partition. In the partition is a door on which is painted in black the last letter of the alphabet of the angels. He opens the door and finds the stall empty, except for a high four-legged stool on which sits an ornately carved cedar box. He opens the box and finds within it two crystal spheres the size of large marbles. He picks them up and examines them. He cannot remember their use. He replaces them in the box and sets the box on the stool and turns his attention to the walls of the stall.

They are completely covered with pictures of varying sizes. The largest are about the size of his hand, the smallest the size of the nail of one of his little fingers. He focuses on one chosen at random. There is the girl in the blue cloak standing at a table in the spiritist shop holding in her hand and closely examining a two-pronged object that he cannot make out, though it looks similar to the one he remembers having seen in the curio shop. He turns to another and sees the man in yellow holding a bunch of blue flowers resembling the wild violets he has seen growing in the curio shop. In another he sees the sandy-haired woman from the first door walking the hallway that leads from the door into her house. The picture has caught her midstep. Her back is to him, and in the foreground of the picture is a large, dark figure that seems to be following her. The figure's back also also is turned to him, and he cannot make out whether it is human or something else. Hanging from a nail on one wall of the hallway, somewhat ahead of the woman, is what appears to be a white garment, and, just beyond the garment, a door. How has he overlooked that door before? On the door is the numeral 3 in brass. He will have to retrace his steps.

He turns to where the door of the stall was, and it is no longer there. He looks all about him. There is no door anywhere. He also notices that there seems to be no source of light in the room, yet he sees with perfect clarity. He finds the picture of the girl in the blue cloak standing in the spiritist shop, but she has moved. She has turned away from the table, and her hand is reaching behind her to replace the two-pronged object. In the distance, unnoticed by the girl, the man in red, the man in yellow, and the man in white stand together, looking toward her. One of them holds before himself a picture frame about two feet square, and within the frame, in black on a white background, is a single glyph: the last letter of the alphabet of the angels.

There are the letter, the ring, the two crystal spheres in the cedar box. Where is the door?

He reaches into the picture and takes hold of the letter with both hands, gripping it like the steering wheel of a cream-colored De Soto he once drove down a country road in summer under a canopy of great leafy trees. He was just previously lying in a field beyond the trees in a bed of yellow flowers, their heavy perfume rising like steam under the steady sun. What was her name? *Legion,* he is sure. He grasps the letter with both hands, but it refuses to move. He lets it go and returns to the cedar box. He opens it, removes the crystal spheres, and holds them to his eyes. The receptionist sits before him behind his counter.

"Congratulations, sir," the receptionist says. "I see you are beginning to recall their use. Your choices have been many, but you have recognized few of them. This is the common experience of men. Her name was Legion, as you remembered. But fear not; I am with you alway."

The vision closes, and he is alone again in the stall. He returns the spheres to the box and puts the box in a pocket of his jacket. He goes to the wall through which he has entered, thrusts his hands into it, and tears it. He steps through into the hallway and walks back in the direction from which he has come. The hostile inhabitants of the stalls are gone now, and scraps of yellowed newspaper blow across darkened streets. He goes back through the second door and feels his way down the stairs to the first and passes back through it. He brushes past the dark, hulking figure without discerning its identity, past the sandy-haired woman who is frozen midstep, past the white garment hanging from the nail, to the door to which is riveted the brass figure of the numeral 3, opens the door, and passes through.

He is standing in a field of grass under a summer sun. The air is warm. At a short distance are the man in red, the man in yellow, the man in white; the first standing erect and looking toward the sun, the second crouching as if to kneel, the third on his knees with his face in his hands. To the right of them is the girl in the blue cloak, holding the two-pronged object in her hands with her head bowed, as if presenting it as an offering to a sacred image. To the right of her, the receptionist sits behind his desk, absorbed in a sheaf of papers. To the right of him the woman whose name was Legion stands on a mound of yellow flowers. Her jeans are cut away to expose her sex, and two holes are cut in her sweatshirt to expose her breasts. Behind him, he knows without looking, is the road that passes under the canopy of trees, and the cream-colored Desoto moving along the road.

"Now we are making progress," he says aloud. He walks up to each of the figures in turn. Each is made of cardboard, supported by a flimsy wooden frame. They remind him of a dream he had as child, of giraffes standing about on a hillside, each made of cardboard supported by a wooden frame. He pushes each figure over in turn with a touch of his hand. They lie in the grass in the sunshine, and he stands with his hands clasped behind his back, gazing across the prairie, waiting for the last letter of the alphabet of the angels to appear over the horizon.

A tale of detection

I

The call from my partner, Dobson, comes shortly after midnight.

"I don't want to spoil the surprise," Dobson says. "You gotta see this for yourself."

It's in a lower middle-class neighborhood, nice houses, nothing special. This house is white, two stories, old. The crime scene is set up when I get there—flashing lights, yellow tape, uniforms all over the place. Dobson stands on the front porch.

"What's happening?" I ask him.

He shakes his head. "Nothing like I've ever seen," he says, "and I thought I'd seen it all."

I follow him through the front door. He touches the shoulder of one of the two uniforms who are standing in front of us, and they make way, and there's Mrs. Brineholt sitting on the living room sofa in red pants and top, rocking back and forth, holding the baby's head to her chest. Just the head. The body is nowhere in sight.

"Jesus, Mary, and Joseph," I say. "What is this?"

Dobson shakes his head again.

"As far as we can figure out, they came home from a movie about eleven-thirty. The babysitter was gone, and the baby's head was sitting on the coffee table. We haven't found the body. A neighbor heard the screaming and called nine-one-one. By the time the first car got here, she was sitting like this, in shock. She won't let us take it away from her, and she won't communicate. There's an ambulance and a shrink on the way. We haven't found the babysitter, either."

"Where's the husband?"

"In the kitchen, looking pretty much like her. There's a uniform with him, too. Come on upstairs. You need to see the baby's room."

I follow him up the stairs.

The room is all pastel pink and yellow and white and blue, very clean and tidy, except for the crib and the floor around it. Evidently the baby was killed in the crib. The blankets are soaked with dark, clotted blood. It has puddled on the plastic mattress cover underneath and trickled down the side at one corner onto the floor.

"The killer must have put the body in some kind of a container, maybe a plastic bag, before he left the crib, because there's not a trace of blood anywhere else in the house. Must have put the head in a bag, too, to take it downstairs."

We go back downstairs. The lab boys are dusting for prints, cameras are flashing, the ambulance has arrived, and the shrink with a hypodermic needle to sedate the Brineholts, who are carried out on stretchers. The medical examiner puts the head in a plastic bag and puts that in a brown paper bag and takes it to the morgue. I give orders for armed guards to be put on the front and back doors twenty-four hours a day until further notice and go home to bed for four more hours.

Morning, Dobson and I are both at the precinct early. He's there first. I pull up a chair close to his desk and say, "Show me what we've got." He takes from a drawer of his desk a brown paper bag much like the one the medical examiner used a few hours ago, which he sets carefully on the desk top. The top of the bag is rolled. He unrolls it deliberately, then reaches inside and takes out and sets on the desk—at this point, memory fails me—either three highly polished silver balls the size of large marbles, or one grossly pornographic postcard addressed "To whom it may concern."

2

In the darkness just before dawn a young woman carrying a white plastic trash bag loaded with a heavy, bulky object approaches a gate in a wall. The wall is made of cinder blocks and is more than eight feet high. The gate is of iron. It has no handle on the outside, only a small square hole covered on the inside. The young woman approaches the gate across a deserted street, looking nervously from side to side.

The gate is set inside the wall about two feet, and the entryway thus formed is darkly shadowed. The young woman steps into the darkness and raps three times on the gate with a small mallet she finds hanging there. The grated window opens immediately and a stern voice says, "What do you want?"

The face behind the grating is invisible in the darkness.

"I'm the babysitter," the young woman whispers. "I've come to deliver the package and get new instructions."

The window cover slams shut with a metallic clink, and the gate begins to open inward, slowly and silently.

The young woman stands holding the white bag at her left side. She is very patient. Before the door has fully opened, the night, a day, and most of another night pass. Meanwhile, flowers from the gardens within the wall slip silently through the opening—hyacinth, iris, snapdragon, yellow daisy, orchid, tulip, daffodil, certain species of Campanula, the entire order Rubiales, one by one, like the notes of a lesser known étude of Chopin played very slowly, and join the procession passing on the street behind her.

This procession has its origin in a distant part of the city, where the players' costumes are manufactured in vile sweatshops situated at appropriate intervals on the banks of rivers, the confluence of which escapes the attention of most cartographers, however appreciative they might be of Chopin, of the craftsmanly murder of infants, of Rubiales, even of the more subtle varieties of alibi concocted by the most desperate criminals.

The procession passes this point on the street at almost the exact same time each morning, though sometimes later. The young woman knows nothing of this, of course, and only considers herself fortunate to witness so artful a display, which she watches by a kind of second sight without having to turn away from the gate. She remains in her place until the last wagon has passed, and her left leg becomes indistinguishable from those of the ivory statues on display in the quarters of the tailors who made the costumes, and the ivy creeps furtively up her inner thigh. The liberties taken by the ivy signal the moment for her to enter the garden.

3

We conduct the interrogation on a tiled area near the fountain. We sit at a small table, the babysitter across from me, Dobson at my left. I place on the table a life-sized Latex model of the body of the infant as we imagine it must have looked in reality, while still intact.

"What do you know about this?" I ask.

"Who are you?" she asks. "Are you here to give me my new instructions?"

Dobson smirks. "Oh, we'll give you instructions, all right."

"What's in the bag?" I ask her, trying to ignore Dobson.

"I think I want to talk to an attorney," she says.

"Oh, we'll get you an attorney all right," Dobson says, continuing to smirk.

"If you won't give me new instructions, then I must show my attorney this," she says, pulling the hem of her dress far up on her left thigh. The leg is completely, thickly enveloped in ivy, almost to the top. My eyes are fixed on the two inches of snowy flesh between the edge of her dress and the top of the ivy. She extends the leg out to the side, until her heel rests several yards away in a patch of hyacinth that has failed to escape with its fellows.

I begin to fear that the case is insoluble, and I arise and walk slowly and sadly out to find the procession, leaving Dobson to his own devices.

4

I enter a small diner at noon, not really expecting to find a seat open, but there is Dobson sitting at the counter with an empty seat at his left. Sitting on the counter in front of him, just beyond his plate, in fact, is the head, still showing not a sign of decomposition. I still marvel at how cleanly it has been cut off, so that it sits there on the stump of the neck as evenly and firmly as a bust of Pythagoras.

I haven't thought of Pythagoras in years.

I sit down beside Dobson.

"Well," I say, "any progress?"

"Plenty," he says. "You left too soon."

"Did she confess?"

"No. She's still holding out. But we expect her to crack any day now."

The head is beginning to undergo a transformation. It grows larger, and the angelic infant features are maturing, grossening. I order a toasted ham and cheese sandwich and watch the transformation progress while I wait. Dobson has already finished his lunch—a double cheeseburger with fries—and is drinking his coffee, holding the cup in two hands with his elbows resting on the counter, looking glumly down at the head. By this time it is that of a large, fat, and bald adult, rather resembling an older Mussolini.

"It keeps doing this," Dobson says. "Last time it was Charles Manson. The time before that it was some old Greek."

"Pythagoras," I say, instantly knowing.

"Yeah, him. How'd you know?"

I have no answer. I am lost in a memory of standing on a beach a long time ago, something like Miami Beach, looking at a lifeguard's tower, where the girl sits holding a baby, and ivy is growing up all about the tower, and from the tower in each direction along the beach as far as I can see is a line of busts of Pythagoras, carved in ivory, resting in the sand and looking toward the sea.

A new job

"We'll start you in the Receiving Department."

I am truly grateful for the job.

"Take this paper through that door and give it to Sheryl. She'll tell you what to do."

I take the paper through the indicated door and find myself in an enormous open bay of desks where young men are working at computer terminals. Line upon line of desks, lines so long I can't see the end of them. Fluorescent lighting, beige and gray walls and floor, acoustical tile ceiling—your standard office, but so many desks.

A young woman sits at a counter to my right. I give her the paper and say, "I'm looking for Sheryl."

"Of course you are," she says, "and you should be truly grateful for the job."

She takes the paper and starts down the aisle between two lines of desks. She pauses to speak to someone, pauses as if to think, turns, pauses, continues on, working her way down the aisle, her dress a patch of blue here, there, moving down the aisle, becoming very small. Then I see that the far end of the office bay is a forest of pines. The blue patch moves into the forest and disappears among the trees.

Standing among the trees, sunlight filtering through the boughs and needles. Before me a building, like a warehouse, one story, concrete and steel, surrounded by a chain link fence with no gate in sight. Over the door a sign: "Receiving Department." The door opens inward, and a young woman steps out wearing blue denims, western boots, a white cotton shirt with the tails tied up to expose a lean abdomen. She leans against the wall to one side of the door with her right elbow resting in her left hand, holding a cigarette on which she draws from time to time. I standing watching her for a long time, wondering if this is Sheryl. All the time I watch her, the sun hardly seems to move.

"Come in," she says eventually, between draws on the cigarette.

There is still no way in, so I go to the right, along the fence line, which turns to my left. I follow the fence to the left for a while until I realize it extends beyond my sight into the forest. I stop and turn to look behind me and see it also extends out of sight the way I've just come. I wonder what to do. The sun is warm through the trees, the pines smell hot, and finally I am so overcome by sleepiness I lie down on the carpet of red, brittle pine needles and sleep.

In a hotel room, looking through the window toward a beach in late afternoon. The shadows are long. At the edge of the beach, silhouetted against the restless water, six giraffes are blazing furiously, great orange and yellow fires.

"I'm looking for . . ." and I stop, not knowing how to finish the sentence. I am speaking to a young woman who stands behind me, to my right. I can't see her, but it is impossible to be unaware of her presence.

"I know," she says, "but I can't help you without more information. So I suggest we stick to questions that can be answered, like 'how long can this go on?'"

The giraffes, who are all standing, writhe and contort, flinging up one leg, then another. Their mouths are open in silent screams. Indeed, how long?

A wind is up, and pennants flutter, blue and yellow. On each is embroidered in white block letters a word of which I can make out only "RY."

Waystation

A small house at the edge of a cliff overlooks a sea. The one door and all the windows have long since been removed by scavengers, but the scavengers are not vandals, and they have left undamaged the true treasure contained within this house: the pictures. The pictures cover the walls and ceilings; the door frames; the cupboards, inside and out; every inch of paintable surface is covered with them. There are undoubtedly many thousands of them, though no one is known to have counted. Some have begun but after several days have recognized the hopelessness of the task. One investigator found that some of the pictures moved to other locations even as he counted them. The pictures are of all sizes, some as large as the stretch of a man's arms and some so small that even with a magnifying glass one can barely make out the scenes depicted. The windows at the back of the house overlook the sea, and as seen through one of the windows the view is always sunlit, the sky always blue, the sea always blue and white-capped, no matter what the time of day or the weather or light conditions as seen from outside. At times the wind sweeps rain throughout the house, but the pictures are miraculously undamaged. The colors have never faded, and in some cases seem actually to have brightened with the passing of years. Once as I stood in the kitchen, looking out toward the sea, I was certain that a woman sat at the table behind me, drinking tea and turning the pages of a volume of verse, but I understood that if I turned she would not be there, so I continued looking out the window. The air was laden with a scent of mowed grass warming in summer sunlight. Later I found a picture of her, about as large as the palm of my hand, sitting at that very table with the very cup of tea and a book, but she was turned slightly away from me and I couldn't see her face. Beside that picture was another of a man walking along a road bordered on either side by a stone wall overgrown with a perfect profusion of roses. He wore a broad-brimmed hat of the kind seen in pictures of Goethe and carried a staff, and he appeared to be moving at a leisurely pace beneath the summer sun. I recognized that road; it passed a mere mile from the cliff's edge. So far as I know I have never met the man himself, although I have sometimes remembered that I myself was the man. I sometimes remember walking leisurely along that road, raising dust in the motionless air, knowing I was approaching the lane that turned toward the house. I don't remember having actually arrived at the house on that journey, and often I remember nothing of the journey at all.

There are several reasons why this won't work

There are several reasons why this won't work. For one, the road extends indefinitely beyond the horizon, down a narrow hallway papered in yellow and hung with the ivory arms of lost infants. For another, a mirror hangs in the air in innumerable particles of glittering dust, remembering vaguely its old place on the wall of a small house in woods, or peering out from among the clotted roots of cedars and spruces. I have tried to explain this, but you know how it is: money is scarce, the weather uncertain, the smell of the spruces under the hot sun heavy in the air. Then the children come, a procession of them, so many, shuffling silently along the yellow corridor, eyes wide and soft and sad, thinking of earlier days when they conversed freely with deer whose antlers were bright with rain. We lie on our bed, propped on our elbows, watching them, hardly conscious of our nakedness, remembering light on ancient seas.

Yellow snakes

A man watches the movements of a yellow snake as thick as his wrist and as long as he is tall. He stands on a strip of broken, weed-grown asphalt, holding a baby cradled in his left arm, with his right hand supporting, the baby loosely wrapped in a pastel blue cotton blanket with a corner laid over his face to protect it from the sun. The heat is becoming oppressive. He smells the asphalt, and the weeds droop.

Rising up from the old asphalt road is an embankment of granite stones the size of the baby's head, an embankment as massive as the face of a great dam. At the top of the embankment, out of sight, beyond the upper edge, is the highway. The baby's mother, who has been the man's wife, waits there, sitting on the shoulder of the highway with her back against the protective barrier. Her back is turned to him; he knows that.

He knows that this country has no venomous snakes; he has heard that; all of his life he has believed that; he remembers that; and he thinks of it as he watches the sinuous tube of yellow emerge from the stones a few yards up the embankment and disappear again among stones a few yards away. There must be mice living under the stones, he thinks. He feels the heat around him rise by degrees. If he does not begin climbing the embankment right away, he will need to find shade, and there is some below the asphalt road, under the trees that grow along a trickle of creek. He could rest there for a while.

But he does not. He begins to pick his way carefully up the stony slope. The tips of thistle leaves emerge tentatively between stones ahead of him. Where there are thistles there may be the yellow snakes, he remembers. He picks his way carefully. The baby beside him holds the little finger of his left hand and tries to keep up, but the man knows it was difficult for him. The asphalt road behind him is becoming crowded with trailer trucks, the great blue boxes rattling their sides together, and he wonders if the woman will wait for him. A snake leaps from between two stones toward his face, and he bats it away with his right hand, startled.

He remembers the first time he saw one of these yellow snakes. It was a long time ago, when he was a boy.

How has he come to be at the bottom of this embankment, standing alongside this broken piece of the old, two-lane highway? He does not remember, though he supposes he must have come over the hills behind him. He has come from somewhere beyond those hills. A fragmentary memory comes to him of carrying the infant through a tangle of tall grass, in the heat of an early August afternoon, watching large yellow snakes as thick as his own thigh squirm slowly away from his steps, his careful, slow steps.

He turns to his left to find his former wife standing beside him, knowing that she simultaneously is sitting with her back against the protective barrier above him, and he says to her, "I'll try to get to you in time. I'll try to get to you before they come. Please wait for me."

"I'll be there," she replies. "There is still time."

And then he is alone. He wonders if it would be easier to drop down across the road and into the ravine. He does so, and standing in the creek in the bottom of the ravine he grasps at a fish with both hands, but it slips away into the reeds; and he looks back up the slope to the highway above, and the woman, now with his own face, and a yellow snake coiled on her lap, looks up and says, "I will wait. There is still time."

On a Thursday

I last saw her in the middle of an afternoon in late June, unseasonably cool, and I was eating a sandwich at a food court in a shopping mall. It was a Thursday. I was alone at a table by a wall, and I saw her walking quickly along the opposite side. She was wearing a white dress printed with small red flowers, also wearing a pale blue sweater and carrying a white purse hanging from her left shoulder. Her hair was cut shorter than usual, but still blonde, held back from her ears by red barrettes. It flounced a bit as she walked, quickly, intently, looking directly forward, not turning her head, and she didn't see me.

The instant I saw her I put down my sandwich and went after her. I called her name, but she seemed to pay no attention, just kept walking. I dodged between the tables as politely as I could, but I couldn't reach her before she turned the corner into the mall concourse. I turned after her and walked fast, careful not to bump into people but hurrying. She kept walking, and I kept following, but I couldn't catch her. She exited the mall by the south exit and continued down the sidewalk. I kept following, but I couldn't seem to move fast enough. We walked on and on, out of the city center, into a rundown section of pawnshops and sandwich counters and adult bookstores and parking garages, then car lots and a Blue Boutique, the Southern Xposure Club for Members Only, then more car lots. We came to where weeds grew up through cracks in the sidewalk, then a vacant lot, then warehouses and wholesale dealers. I was nearly a block behind her when she suddenly cut across the street—a deserted street—and went through the door of a large, high, windowless and nameless building. I followed her across and through the door, and I was in a large open bay filled with desks and computer terminals and keyboard operators. The ceiling was high, and the bay was lighted by bright fluorescent lamps. She walked down an aisle between desks, and I followed behind, and she went through a door at the back of the room, and I followed, and as I passed through the door I saw as in a vision the immensity of the place, buildings and parking lots and more buildings, and she was out there somewhere, and I walked on frantically, desiring to smell her perfume on that blue sweater and feel its softness against my face again.

Banners of past lives

We departed early, raising banners of past lives before us. The road lay through a run-down subdivision on the edge of the city, a place where housewives still hung clothes on lines to dry. One wore a dark blue dress with a low hem and long sleeves, and a light-blue bandanna around her head and a white apron. She kept the clothespins in a large pocket on the apron. Her husband, who had lost an arm in combat, sat inside in the breakfast nook reading a newspaper and drinking lukewarm coffee. It was necessary for him to lay down the paper each time he wanted to pick up his cup. They still made love, however, usually in the woman-astride position, though occasionally in the "crayfish." When he heard the commotion raised by our passing, the husband came to the doorway to watch, wearing the expression of a man remembering a past life, a life of gallantry and glory in long-past wars, in that southern country where the housewives are often trapped in the walls, moving about silently in the dark spaces.

We were tired. The previous night we had ascended and descended stairways endlessly, remaining resolutely cheerful but tired. We always were tempted to open one of the doors that we occasionally passed on the stairways, hoping to find a comfortable place to lie down, but rest came rarely to us—it was necessary to keep moving as long as possible, though there was no definite requirement, only a sense of inescapable duty. We therefore departed early, raising the banners of past lives.

At a rest stop, we sat at picnic tables in the shade of cottonwood trees and watched the travelers stroll on the grass and consider their plans. The place was infested with snakes, mottled red and yellow snakes about twelve inches long. They were being called "coral snakes," though I knew that was incorrect. They had short, needle-sharp teeth and the ability to leap into the air fully extended, the tip of the tail attaining to one or two inches above the ground. They caused much apprehension, but there was reason to believe that they were not venomous. A young man whom I knew to be somewhat impulsive in his behavior was playing with one of them, teasing it, pulling at its tail, holding it and shifting it from hand to hand. "I hope you will let that go," I said to him, and he replied, "I want to do this." The previous night, I had passed him on the stairs, and it had occurred to me then that he might be troublesome.

Homecoming

I recall a large hole excavated through the asphalt of a street; a yellow inflatable raft imbedded in the gravelly earth at one side of it; for some reason the road workers had left it exposed. We had buried that raft there two years before because it had a leak we couldn't patch and the city hadn't yet supplied us with trash barrels, then the street had been put through and our secret covered over by asphalt. Before coming upon it, I had found it necessary to ascend through a flowing creek that spread out over a slope, ankle deep in water. I could have stepped to the side into shallower water, but it was swifter there, over larger and possibly slippery gravel, and even with my walking stick I preferred to avoid the risk. At the top of the slope was a large patch of grass and weeds, then a wood fence with a gap, and beyond the gap I found myself back in the subdivision. That was where I came on the hole in the asphalt, with the inflatable raft, near our house. But I have neglected to mention the snakes. Lying at the top of the slope was a four-foot section of tree trunk, perhaps a foot in diameter, weathered smooth and gray. As I put one foot over it, I saw a snake stretched out on the ground just in front of me, patterned like a rattlesnake, a good three feet long, but no thicker than my index finger, with a narrow head, immediately identifying it as nonvenomous, but it was bad tempered, striking out at my walking stick. I fended it off with the stick, and it slipped under the log and went on its way. Then another snake emerged suddenly from a hole in the ground, this one considerable thicker, perhaps two inches, black with yellow and red rings. I immediately thought "coral snake," but the order of the coloring was wrong. What struck me about this specimen was what looked very much like blonde hair on its head, long enough to be combed back and parted. I allowed it to exit its hole and vanish into the weeds a few feet away. It was then that I passed through the weeds (taking care to probe ahead of me with my stick for the snake) and then through the gap in the fence into the subdivision, where a woman holding the second snake expected me.

A DOOR STANDS OPEN, BEYOND IT THE SUN

A door stands open, beyond it the sun; people walking in and out, through the door into the sun, from the sun through the door, figures in black silhouette; a door like any ordinary door in a house, a door with knobs. I am lying, half conscious, unable to feel my legs, on the bed with the iron stead that sits against a wall of the hallway where people pass, going and coming. An indistinct form appears beside the bed, a hand touches my head, and a voice as if coming from a great distance says, "Rise up, and walk," and I rise from the bed to walk with those who come from the sun, down a winding staircase to the street outside to mingle with the swirling throngs.

I try a shop door and it opens. A meeting is in progress—the seven members of the Disaster Preparedness Committee sit around a U-shaped conference table, three members on each arm of the U facing each other, the chairman sitting at the bottom of the U facing the door that I have just opened. I stand, uncertain what to do. The chairman looks up at me, and then all the other members turn to look.

"Please take a seat," the chairman says, and I take a chair against the wall to one side. It occurs to me that I have some responsibility connected with this committee. A strange feeling comes over me, with the shadow of a memory—I have been here before.

I have difficulty following the discussion, my mind wanders, and I catch only a few words and phrases: "imminent," "utmost urgency," "possibly beyond our resources," "the bridge," "burial teams."

Then the chairman turns to me again and asks, "Does all of this meet with your approval? Do you have any further directions for us?"

I am surprised, but I sense that the safest answer for me to give is, "Yes, yes, of course. Keep me informed. I will issue new directives as necessary."

That seems to satisfy the committee members, and they all stand and disperse, leaving me alone in my chair. I envision the ground quaking outside and fissures opening to reveal multicolored strata of earth and rock, and in the depth of the largest fissure the white light of the sun.

Trail descends and narrows

Trail descends and narrows
Not like this on the ascent
Rock face on right
Deep water on left
Rock face overhanging trail
Impossible to pass upright
It has changed
Easier on the ascent
Leaning backward over water
Clinging to rocks
Stepping sideways
Uncertain handholds
On quartz and granite
Crumbling
Overhang of rock face is lower
Trail narrows
Hanging backward over water
Over chasm
Would be worse with pack
Safe ground and trees
Just beyond crumbling rock

A sphere grows inside my breast

A sphere grows inside my breast
Green and smooth
It begins quite small, steadily enlarges
Until it no longer fits inside my body
I do not feel it, there is no pressure
The spreading surface passes through my organs
    and beyond my skin
Painlessly, silently
I would not notice it did I not see it in the vision of the mind
Is this a bad thing, or a good thing?
Is there cause for alarm?
How far will it go?
Beyond my house?
Beyond the earth?
Beyond the solar system and outward?
It reminds me of spheres I remember in paintings by Magritte
Resting on the ground among houses, as large as houses
People go about their business as if the spheres were not there
Perhaps it is better to ignore them
Their existence poses unsettling questions
As the sphere continues to grow
I will go fishing
To a small lake in woods
Hidden among dark firs
I will fish with artificial flies
Cast out among lily pads
The water lilies are in bloom, yellow

Looking Down a Narrow Valley

Looking down a narrow valley where a river runs straight
Both sides heavily wooded with fir and spruce
A notch of clear sky in the distance where the river drops
    over the horizon
Hanging in the notch against the blue sky
An enormous boulder of weathered limestone
Carved with letters of a language I do not know
They are scripture of a vanished race
I touch the carvings with my finger tips
Tiny grooves
A long step from the top of the boulder to the left ridge
    of the canyon
But the air among the trees is sweet
The odor of fir and spruce needles warmed by the sun
The vision of the unknown alphabet is clear in the memory
As I sit cross-legged in the mouth of a cave
Behind me in hooded robes, some of blue and some of red
Are the members of a band of itinerant scholars
Or perhaps they are workmen, or jugglers
They are very small
Letters of the unknown alphabet scratched into the walls
    of the cave
On the ceiling and the walls
And a drawing of an unknown animal
An animal with long legs and a hornless head
It speaks slowly but its words cannot be made out
The girls who attend it are gowned in diaphanous gauze

That would catch fire if exposed to the sun
One of them points at letters on the wall
And gazes back expectantly, as if waiting for a response
But in the distance the river flashing in code demands attention
The small men in red and blue are dispersed among the trees
Birches have grown up among the firs
Smooth pebbles exude from small holes in the bark
And slide in orderly streams down the trunks
Pebbles red and blue
A letter carved on each of them
The boulder fragments as if from within
The pieces move apart slowly
Blue sky appears between them
They cease to move
The cluster holds its position
The girls approach from behind
Careful to remain in shade
The key to the unknown language is kept in a box
At the back of the cave
One of the girls sits on it
The other moves a finger on the wall, writing

Pregnant moving vans jostle together on the highway

Pregnant moving vans jostle together on the highway
The flowing hair of the lead truck sinks into the summer sun like
    fishing line
Bread falling in cubes from the power lines overhead
Assembles itself into braided ropes
They strangle the doves of minimal efficiency
That carpet the pavement in slow imitation of musical chairs
Meanwhile the very thin wife of the local police chief
Bares her wrists to display in a shop window
The blue tattoos of an atrophied love

The doves of minimal efficiency

The doves of minimal efficiency cling tenaciously
    to their ancient privileges
Inking their maps on the walls of abandoned police stations
Composing music under the shelter of desert camouflage
Storing their eyes at night in small cedar boxes
When not observing through slits in the ceilings
    the movement of armies

The apex of an isosceles triangle

The apex of an isosceles triangle etched behind the cornea
    of a carp's eye
Trembles like a severed lip cowering in the interstice
    of a moth's wing and A flat
While the sun sleeps untroubled between the breasts
    of the Shulamite
With a pre-dynastic king-list carved in bas-relief below her navel
Apple blossoms erupt from all the hair of her body

Fishhooks tied to silken filaments

Fishhooks tied to silken filaments
Trail behind words like dogs circling to make their beds
Or the odor of dreams
Dragged through streets after rain
Such are the ruminations of the tenured philosophers
Who stroll among photographs of aging porn stars
Talking of spider webs that drift across the corpses
    of unicorns and poets
The subtle modeling of which illustrates eons of hope and
    hesitation

Walking in the shadow of the sun's memory

Walking in the shadow of the sun's memory
I pause to brush away the leaves from inside my face
The notes of last night's concerto swollen with rage
Crashing against a cliff's face
Exploding brains of bison
That lately wandered the streets of a deserted city
The brains exude the odor of a woman's breath

The delicate music of the spheres

The delicate music of the spheres that grow in the breasts
    of street magicians
Conjures wars out of a thin line of memory
As the mathematics of lunacy leaks from the moon's fear
And fills the air with groans of dying strategy
The wars emit a music of their own
That inspires gangs of urchins who drag boats
    through empty boulevards
And run their fingers along the corner line of every wall and ceiling
Seeking a path to the sea

The indecision of a lark's tongue

The indecision of a lark's tongue
Licking the inner thigh of a weeping statue
The statues weep throughout the city for the children lost
Wandering the plain through misted blood

Dawn breaks crimson from the music box

Dawn breaks crimson from the music box
Its color tinges the face
Of the woman of papier mâché hands who looks out the window
The border of her robe drapes the floor and the furniture
The robe of forest-green velvet
Its hem is a chain of glass cubes
They have been dragged through the shimmer of kisses
That spreads across the valley below the window
When you kiss her her lips are wooden bannisters
Of stairways in hunting lodges where Blue Beard composes music
The music box plays one of his lullabies
When you touch the woman's hand it breaks off
Fragments of paper float up from the stub
They are engraved with secrets in cypher even she does not know
She begins to sing
Her song is a guillotine blade
That divides the kisses evenly among her lovers

A dream wrapped in rain wrapped in a dream

A dream wrapped in rain wrapped in a dream
Stands naked shivering outside the shrine
Contemplates the procession through the night
Of white and red and cobalt blue
And writes equations on falling snow

The day arrives late

The day arrives late
Disheveled as having hastily left a lover
Her gown unhooked absentmindedly
To reveal between her shoulder blades
A window facing on a neglected garden
Where burnt corpses of invading metaphysicians provide cover
    for children
To play hide-and-seek with the queen's chief torturer
Who secretly conspires with the hovering dust raised
    by vanished horsemen
To tattoo inside her right thigh an image of her left thigh

The tumescent orchid that lies ignored on the altar

The tumescent orchid that lies ignored on the altar
Recalls a time past
When legs of brittle newspaper
Supported a bedspring between the gate pillars of the temple
That was before the packs of coyotes with the hide torn
    from their chests
Before the concubines of the high priest
And then the news of a train derailed in the remote Himalayas
Floating for one ecstatic moment
A spider's filament glinting sunlight
Before hurtling into an abyss of piano keys and velvet

The piano keys melt slowly in the afternoon sun

The piano keys melt slowly in the afternoon sun, but inexorably,
Recalling the flow of spiced honey through long and white fingers
And onto the nylon-stockinged thighs of a dreaming poetess.
She picks raspberry seeds from between her teeth and plants them on the ivories,
Dropping them one by one into holes pried open by a darning needle in the hand of an armless mannequin.
I watch from under the wallpaper,
Taking care not to draw attention to myself.
The pistol in my right trouser pocket, however,
Sends forth green sprouts that become entangled in the works of all the clocks in the palace.
I urge it telepathically to be more discreet,
But it holds itself aloof from all direct interaction with human beings.
The poetess rouses herself from her languor to hover above the keyboard of the piano.
The keys are the petals of blossoming lies;
Her fingers flutter in them, attempting to coax out a note or two.

A THREAD OF LIGHT FLOATS

A thread of light floats in a darkened hallway
The walls poised and wary
Breath slow as the sap
In the lilacs growing from the roof

Though I feared we might find happiness together

Though I feared we might find happiness together
A convocation of wood lice absconded with the letters of our poem
Where now is the sunlight that escaped between the curtains of your face?
Where the white rabbits that frolicked on the small of your back?
One of your breasts was a fallow deer swimming against the current of the Nile
The other a locked room storing souvenir bus tokens from before the war
To think of you is to be trapped on a stairway between walls of fire
Hearing the distant performance of a Scarlatti mass
As a white rabbit descends the stairs
Trailing dreams of sunflowers

I KEEP YOUR KISSES IN A BOX

I keep your kisses in a box
I take them out to count them in the long evenings
When memories tiptoe furtively across the walls
I keep them in a paper box that once held chocolates
    wrapped in foil
Red and blue and gold and silver
The kisses rattle when I shake the box
They were not so small and hard when you gave them to me

I hide in the deep grass of my heart

I hide in the deep grass of my heart
All the women I have loved are oval mirrors
Standing silent sentinel along the walls of a hallway
They will see me if I move
Their eyes are my nipples in turns through the long night
I must not look at them
An enemy moves silently along the hallway
Looking this way and that, rifle at the ready
I carefully part the grass with my hands
In a moment of inattention the enemy walks into
    one of the mirrors
But only part way, part of him remains outside the mirror
He seems to be trapped
The grass is water draining between my fingers

The Twisted Rope of Day

The twisted rope of day falls in a heap on the floor
I hide in a fetal position in the box that hides inside your ribs
Last night I opened the door of your left breast and removed
    a clock
It sits covered by a cape of swans' beaks on a chest of drawers
It hides from the wolf of cracked glass
That slithers about the room against the walls
I float backward through the wood of the box
Through your ribs
Through your skin
I stand naked on the window sill
I am the shadow of irresolution
I am the minute hand of the clock
Your kisses are snowflakes that swirl about me
When the river in which the swans bathe splits into three paths
    into the trees
The wolf of cracked glass removes the swans' beaks in the presence
    of strangers
Who come from the woods dragging their metaphysics
    behind them
Your kisses are whiter than wolf's teeth evanescing
    through the window
The door of a swan's breast opens inward
On a room where a woman transforms herself into a box
    of umbrellas
They are painted with scenes of last night's love
Your kisses are eyes watching from my skin
They are strangers lecturing on metaphysics

Such happiness is rare

Tangled filaments of memory
The intense wiring of a clear mind
Glitter in moonlight on the plain of remorse
A fox's teeth play musical chairs under the stars
Faces peer out from within walls
Then hide beneath a stair
Such happiness is rare
I will go, I will sing
With the merchants of string
Who roll on the floors through well lighted halls
Of ivy and swamp gas and exploding aeroplanes
Such happiness is rare
We will frolic on the plain thick with fleas
That lick the toes of Belgian burlesque dancers
To celebrate the night of the long knives
Protruding like grass from the bellies of wolves
The knives are very fragrant
I roll my nylon stockings down
They collapse with fatigue on quivering blueprints
Of structures of varnished wood and painted letters
I stand in a street in heavy traffic
In the heat of an August afternoon
Your breath is damp on my neck
Such happiness is rare

As an automobile soars off a cliff's edge

As an automobile soars off a cliff's edge
There is still time for the clown who is driving to adjust his makeup
The couple making out in the back seat look up surprised by the
    sudden rise in the pit of the stomach
"Carpe diem," one of them says, and they go back to their business
Unknown to the occupants of the vehicle its launching over the
    cliff is the signal
For an army deployed in the valley below to begin its attack
As soon as the commanding general can remember the objective
The intelligence officer in charge of the sitmap has thought that he
    was playing Risk
As it turns out, the automobile makes a soft landing
After exiting the young man tucks a Risk board under his arm
And begins what he knows will be a long wearisome slog
Through miles of tangled underthings

A book of lamentations

I

How doth the city sit solitary
                      —Lamentations 1:1

How doth the City sit solitary
One white arm thrust out of the broken plaza
Grasping toward the sky
Deserted temples surround the plaza
Darkness within their portals
Pillars white as the arm
The City lies spread behind the mind
The river spread out, dark water
Heads bobbing toward the sea
Deserted piers, warehouses, factories along the riverbanks
Small shops where masks once were made
For processions of acrobats and soothsayers
Dancing through the boulevards
To the unrestrained songs of murdered dogs
While copulating in the shadow of the shrine
Couples as ardent as butterflies' wing dust
Left the imprints of their bodies on the dissolving marble
And where is the girl who opened the cupboard below her breasts
To let spill the glyphs of Abraham's last Apocalypse
An unidentified finger tracing one by one
The bones of her spine and the knobs of the cupboard doors
To lie with her the empty robe of the high priest

Would sacrifice one by one
The threads of which the soothsayer by the river wove it
And therein is the reason why the soothsayer's liver is poured upon the earth
His grief greater than that of a cedar tree bereft of its bones
As it reaches futilely for the hand through the veil
And the head of the king
Scraps of yellowed newspaper sewed to his tongue
Grins through the shattered windshield of a decaying automobile
At rest in the dry grass that grows between the legs of a broken statue
Of the girl who lost the glyphs
The king and the soothsayer yearn to be obeyed again
By the refugees scattered across the plain
Who hang their cooking pots on tripods constructed of discarded windshield wipers
And think of the faces that saw through the veil
The wedding ceremony of the girl who lost the glyphs

2

How hath the Lord cast down the daughter of Zion
with a cloud in his anger,
and cast down from heaven unto the earth the beauty of Israel

—Lamentations 2:1

Cast down from heaven unto the earth
The City is unrecognizable to the legless children who float above the streets
Between the dark-windowed skyscrapers of the previous age
Searching for lost memories that hide

Somewhere heaped up like discarded fast-food containers
They lost their legs in encounters with discredited theories
That fell one by one from the last rainbow
That was before the sea rolling over in its sleep like a
 post-coital angel
Flooded the earth with rationalizations

3

Behold in this horn were eyes like the eyes of man,
and a mouth speaking great things
                    —Daniel 7:8

The horn half buried in a patch of dandelions
Proliferating on the ceiling of the king's apartment
Has the eyes of a man and a mouth speaking great things
Its eyes look down upon the king
Who leafs through the pages of a coffee table book
A compilation of illustrated reports of the steady encroachment on
 his kingdom
By the floating hoards of legless children
He especially likes the pictures painted in the manner of Utrillo's
 early watercolors
He shows one to his favorite concubine
Who sits beside him sorting buttons in the dresser drawers that are
 her eyes
Red ones to the left, yellow ones to the right
Occasionally a few words incomprehensible to the king issue from
 the mouth of the horn
The concubine especially likes the buttons that are the color of the
 dandelions

4

Better is the sight of the eyes than the wandering of the desire
                    —Ecclesiastes 6:9

Better is the sight of the eyes
Than tents of grass erected on the soft flesh of the moon
They burst into flame at the merest touch of a coyote's breath
The eyes ask little of the moon
Though the daily labor of sweeping the corners of a coyote's den
With a fan of earrings
Becomes tedious in the early hours
When a fingernail inscribing small circles on a lover's hip
Drifts into fitful sleep
It dreams of a hallway that opens onto a busy street
Flashing windshields grit blowing in hot wind right turn only
    Mexican Grill I-90 1 Mile
1XU P41 will work for food green arrow coyote broken in the
    gutter

5

Moreover the profit of the earth is for all: the king himself is served by the field
                    —Ecclesiastes 5:9

The king himself is served by the field
Of sequined lilies that spreads itself out on a sheet of graph paper
But he fades in and out with modulations of jazz guitar
The king finds this disconcerting

He takes consolation by resting his hand on a thigh of morning haze
Sheets of graph paper slip discreetly between the guitar notes
But the king snatches them out
Hides them under the hazy thigh

6

And should not I spare Nineveh, that great city?
—Jonah 4:11

The serpent coiled beneath my diaphragm has passed a sleepless night
It looks restlessly this way and that
If I lie motionless it may slip away along the bones of my arm and out a fingertip
And so I lie on my back and watch the oval discs that drift about the room
They are memories of lost loves and interrupted kisses
One rotates gracefully on its vertical axis and exits through an open window
I press myself backward against the underside and watch the landscape slide away below
If the serpent departs here it will fall helplessly undulating
That would amuse me
On the upper side of the disc out of my sight is a forgotten cityscape of Monsù Desiderio
On the base of the principle monument is painted the face of the last queen
If you draw near she will insert her tongue into your mouth
And in gratitude permit you to caress with the tip of your own tongue

The inner surfaces of all her teeth
That prospect evokes a memory of a warm day in a flowering
    pear grove
I shall not speak of it
Meanwhile the discs in my room tire of their movement and rest
    themselves against a wall
Each an unsmiling portrait
My disc leans itself against the inner wall of the city
I step down from it to walk hand in hand with two members of
    the procession
That issues from within the half-melted mansion of
    Monsù's widow
She devotes her days to embroidering her legs with conjugations of
    obsolete verbs
I note that the city wall is built of the teeth of the last queen
Where against it is one permitted to press one's forehead to pray?
I sit in the shade of a vine on a hillside above the city
The serpent is coiled in the grass beside me finally asleep
But by a kind of telepathy we converse at length
He is of the opinion that the current regime has lost the mandate
    of heaven
And I incline to agree
But prefer to contemplate the hypothetical eruption
    in the ruined streets
Of pear blossoms in silent incessant convulsion

Looking for the Captain

"Look," I say to a woman whom I love but who I am not sure loves me. "Look," I say. Mushroom clouds, small, indicating that they were at a great distance, are faintly visible in the black sky, just above the horizon. I look about us; people are milling, talking, arguing, gesticulating. No one else seems to notice the clouds. "When they notice, there will be chaos," I say. "We must find the captain." The captain is an officer deserving of respect. He is a man of good sense and the only one who might be able to keep order when the chaos threatens. The woman—a girl, really, a girl with shoulder-length hair and clothed modestly in a dress of white deerskin—nods in agreement, and we set out. We look first in the dining hall, but the captain is not there. We ask for him by name in the lounge, but no one has seen him. I watch the girl from the corner of my eye, but she does not look back. She is quite lovely, I think, and I wish she would take my hand. I notice how the dress clings to the front of her body. We ascend the rocky face of a cliff and rest near the edge, but not for long. An automobile careens down the slope above us and explodes as it goes over the edge, the debris falling into the valley below. A second one does the same. We move away from the edge into a nearby patch of pines, hoping to find protection from the enemy automobiles, but there is little. A handsome young man whose wife is in the area says, "Are you with us? We need to move you on; it isn't safe here." He stands at the edge of the cliff with me, and we gaze together into the valley, at the bottom of which is dense tropical forest. "Most people enter the valley at one end or the other and don't get much further in," the young man says. "I prefer to explore the center. So does the captain." I stand looking down into the valley, wondering if the girl is near. I consider with a sense of some urgency the alternative routes into the center.

Let there be light

"Let there be light"
And there is darkness
(Lao Tzu knows about it)
It comes out of the forest
Through the trees
As uncertain
As faltering
As a broken-footed revolver
"Then let us go fishing," a man said
(The man in the Stetson hat)
"Let us paddle across the river in the summer sun"
Because the bridge is down
The bridge wraps itself around the legs of old women and
    young girls
Melting in the sun's heat
Like wax flowing from the wings of Icarus
The wax runs down a fire chute
And through the fingers
The sun rolls down the highway
A brass disk
Making a sound of embroidered violins
Grown from the calyx of a white orchid
Its thighs are clasped about your head
The old woman arrives carrying a lantern
The old woman who explains everything
If you put a coin over each of her eyes
She plays the piano on an iceberg like nobody's business

The old woman guards the explanations
She wraps her legs in castoff watercolors
To ward off the dreams that issue from her dried sex
Each dream is a fugitive shadow of hope
For the better times depicted in the discarded paintings
The bridge is down
The skyscrapers curl into themselves
They are crayons, melting
The cranes flying overhead
The five white cranes in a diamond formation
Transmit telepathic reports of distant wars
Working my way laboriously through the tangled girders
    of the bridge
I pick up crayons as I go
Windshields flash from the busy street across the river
Windshields decorated with decals of white cranes
A map of the former city is drawn between my beloved's breasts
    with a black crayon
We walk hand in hand through a corridor in a
    collapsing skyscraper
It is a corridor through the forest
The walls are green-leafed trees
Small snakes rest coiled on the branches
My lover's thighs are pressed together
A box of coiled wires rests in her pubic hair
The wires become a key
The old woman knows what it opens

Lingering over a page of Genesis

Lingering over a page of Genesis
The author was dealing with other problems
Other flowers viewed through a wall by x-ray vision
Flowers with broad sword-like petals
Reminiscent of river banks where tall girls walk
Unstitching themselves slowly for lovers who watch
    from the rushes
Unstitching themselves with delicate movements
Pretending to be oblivious
Other times, other problems
Looking out the window with a finger marking the place:
"Let the waters be gathered together in the womb of the Queen
Of unstitched fingers scattered on the river bank"
Why has no one else ever noticed that line?

Peel the walls away from the brain

Peel the walls away from the brain
The brain an orange
The sections come apart in the hand
The woman standing in the brain scans the horizon
    for threatening ravens
A raven plucks a section from the brain, sucks out the juice
A traveler by the seashore thrusts a hand into the sun
Ravens billow from the wound
Followed by gouts of the sun's blood
Orange
The sun, the sun
Come from the sun, reach into the sun
Thrust a hand into the sun
Born inside the sun
Contain the sun
When the wall splits the sunlight bursts in
The sun contained within the rib cage leaks between the ribs
Lie down on the floor among scurrying small snakes
They do not like the sun
They lick the ribs
They do not like the taste
Paint a picture on the wall with the sun's blood
Orange

BLUE HAND YELLOW HAND

Blue Hand Yellow Hand
Lie open on beach
Blue Hand lifts tangle of kelp
Water drains away
Yellow Hand caresses hip of bathing girl
Blue Hand Yellow Hand
Rest on offshore rocks
Water rises
A river to the sun

The moon swollen in late pregnancy

Moon swollen in late pregnancy
Floats distractedly among cedars
Watched with curiosity by whispering stones
Who themselves drift on a current of broken light
As Old Woman
Who can explain it all
Sleeps dreamlessly in the darkness under the trees
The stones debate how matters have come to such a pass
While fragments of light sink through the viscera
Of the nearly forgotten towers that guard the forest
Their feet anchored securely in the memory of ancient wars
And the melodious mathematics of lost causes
Moon presses her hands to lift her heavy belly
And waits for Old Woman to awake
When she awakes Moon will inquire of her
How the light was shattered
What was at issue in the wars
That haunt the memories of the guardian towers
What will issue from her womb
What will become of the forest
After her blood and water irrigate its roots

Passing through the aspen grove beating hand drums

Passing through an aspen grove beating hand drums
The Singers wear shirts of white elk hide
The shirts are white as the aspen bark
The Singers descend in the night
Sent down by Moon
Moon Woman white as the aspen bark
Sends them down
The leaves are green
They will be yellow, they will be red
The Singers sing of the ancient wars
They sing of the blood that sank to the roots
The blood of the warriors
The blood of Moon Woman who gives birth
The leaves take the color of their blood
The leaves take the color of her blood
The leaves are green (now)

A NEARLY FULL MOON RISING BEHIND THE MOUNTAINS

A nearly full moon rising behind the mountains
Casts doubt on all the philosophy that rises in mists from the lake
Where hover suspended in the deeper water discarded masks
And wasted opportunities
Lying on one's back in the warm mud of the lake bottom
Looking upward through the dark water past the masks and the
    opportunities at the blurred image of the moon
One thinks of a red disk that lies on the bottom nearby
It vibrates with the passing of the breezes above
The letters inscribed on it are sometimes dark and sometimes
    bright and not always legible
It has been said that they mean this:
"The armies will march across the walls like pencil marks
    left by mice.
There is no reason why the sun cannot kneel and genuflect before
    the moon,
But she does not hold it against him that he does not.
Dragonflies nest in the hearts of dandelions,
Or dandelions in the hearts of dragonflies;
The experts disagree."

Cut a slit on the surface of the lake

Cut a slit on the surface of the lake
Pull back the sides like sheet rubber
Darkness bubbles up from the water
It stains the fingers
Ink to smear words on the walls of the cave
Where hide the daughters of the old woman who knows the stories
They huddle dispersed among the boxes
Baring glass teeth borrowed from glass foxes
That lurk in the brittle grass
That grows on the banks of the narrow river
It flows from the lake
It cuts deeper by the year through many-colored strata
Of petrified memory
Of musty garments discarded by the old woman's lovers
Of spiral stairwells with bannisters of foxes' vertebrae
That vanish at infinity
They have many landings along the way
On one sleeps the memory of a couple whose faces are unclear
Legs entangled in legs
A kiss on one breast
On the other an eye opening suddenly in surprise
It sees a vision of young deer
That frolic in a sunlit clearing unmindful of the scarlet battalions
That pass between them and around them like warm water
    through an enlacement of fingers
The young deer
They are those two children

Who disobediently stained their lips and tongues with the juice of
  a certain berry
And her lips became comely with rows of jewels
And he became the tower of David builded for an armoury
Meanwhile the scarlet battalions march down the narrow river
Through the many-colored strata and the heaps of
  discarded garments
Through the narrow canyon toward the cities of the plain

On these two prongs of a deer's antler

On these two prongs of a deer's antler
Hang all the songs of the daughters
Who dwell in the labyrinths beneath the lake
They are legion
They hold between thumb and forefinger
Smooth clear stones
Each with a name written on it

White Mask People and Yellow Mask People

White Mask People and Yellow Mask People
They appear in the aspen groves
Standing together in groups
Watching impassively from among the trees
The masks are oval-shaped and flat
With two slits for eyes and a slit for the mouth
The people are dressed in white tunics with long sleeves
They live in caverns deep in the earth
Where they sit on boxes
Never sleeping
Never needing sleep
They leave the caverns occasionally
To walk and stand among the aspen trees
And sometimes to drift between the moon and the sun
Remembering flights among the stars
One of them writes on the walls of a cavern
He writes by the light of shining stones
Embedded in the rock of the ceiling
He writes with a stylus of raven quill
Dipped in the darkness that is stored in the boxes
The boxes are of cedar
It is very fragrant

A woman stands before an open window

A woman stands before an open window
A breeze agitates the folds of her gown
Her right arm hangs loose at her side holding a white mask
She watches the scarlet army marching through the valley below
I know that her breasts are free beneath the gown
I know the color of the aureoles
I am a music box on her dressing table
I am a seascape on her wall
I am a letter in the drawer of her escritoire
I am a spider hiding in a corner of the floor

Beyond the furthest ridge

Beyond the furthest ridge
A door into summer
Mermaids pirouette on the linoleum in a patch of sunlight
Where an automobile mechanic lies sleeping curled like a crayfish
With my fingertips I feel the ridges and mountains on a map
Seeking a route for the rivers of desire that flow from beneath
    the temple
To give the mermaids a way to return to the sea

A GIANTESS PEELS BACK THE SKIN OF THE EARTH

A giantess peels back the skin of the earth with a fingernail
A clown's face grins through the opening
They are in collusion
To defraud of their maidenhood the girls who pass by fours
 through train stations
The girls' feet do not touch the floor
Though they are not as innocent as they seem
They have learned from old books the secrets the giantess
 will not share
They sometimes sit reading together in a garden in white
 wicker chairs
Enjoying the sunshine and comparing notes
The giantess enjoys immunity from prosecution for her frauds
That fact is noted in one of the books
In a caption to a line drawing
Illustrating the defeat of the legions of the last king
He is the clown who grins through the opening
Where the earth's skin is torn
The fingernail is long and is sometimes employed as a lingam
In an ancient worship of which the girls are secretly priestesses
How all this began is explained in the last chapter of a book of
 which they have heard
But in all their researches have not found

At the end of the evening

At the end of the evening the performers lay their folded costumes
    in the center ring
The ringmaster dallies with a sapphire that impersonates
    a hollow tree
The diagrams carved into its bark resemble sewing patterns
Printed on flimsy paper that aspires to a higher oblivion
The sapphire dissolves with a contented sigh
Its vapor clinging to the clothes of the ringmaster
All its tongues convulsing in unison to the whispers of the
    abandoned costumes
The performers descend a jeweled stairway
That ends as a twist of yellow paper like a fly strip drawn out from
    its container
They will spend most of the night in wondering admiration
    of the diagrams

The undone hair of satisfied desire

The undone hair of satisfied desire
Rises to the surface of the river
On a nearby hill workmen construct a watchtower
Of which each brick and board is a fragment of seerstone
Each stamped with a glyph translatable as I AM
It is to guard a sanctuary for penitent tax collectors
    of the late regime
A strand of hair is trapped in the mortar
But secretly plans to escape disguised as the neck ribbon of a
    visiting laundry girl
One of those who sleep in orderly formations beneath the bottom
    of the river
The weather is especially fine
Hammer blows resound in the summer air

SEVEN TRAILS

On one trail from an opening in woods
A pool of clear water
In the depth a left arm clothed in the sleeve of a white gown
On the pointing finger a gold ring set with an emerald
Carved in the image of a moth
On the second a dying unicorn
Entrails spilled on the grass
And spangled with five-pointed stars red blue and silver
On the third a weathered shack with windows removed
Inside a bed with bare springs
A white porcelain pan upturned on the floor
A girl standing in the doorway
Hugging about her a blanket of moth wings
On the fourth a wrecked library
Books spilled in chaos on the floor
One open to a color plate of De Witte's "Morning Music"
A bouquet of daffodils in place of the pianist's head
On the fifth a steam locomotive abandoned on a stony beach
On the sixth a puppet stage
An enactment of the Book of Genesis in progress
To an audience of recently resurrected unicorns
On the seventh a door that opens to the touch
Releasing clouds of red blue and silver stars

Quartet

The waters shall be healed

—Ezekiel 47:8

I

I stand in the hallway uncertain what to do. Today is the first day of classes—I am returning to university—and I know I have classes, but I have misplaced my schedule and do not know where to go. I see a door to what appears to be an office and go in to inquire. Several people are working there, evidently mostly professors preparing Several people are working there, evidently mostly professors preparing to teach. There are many paper folders and ring binders with tabbed dividers. No one looks up at me. Then a woman approaches.

"Can I help you?" she says.

"Have you ever had that dream about knowing you have classes to attend, but you have lost your schedule and don't know where to go? I am having that experience now."

"Oh, dear. I will see what I can do."

She steps away, speaks to this person and that. Her dress is thin and clings to her hips and breasts. Meanwhile, I attempt to catch glimpses of the ring binders that lie open on the counters, hoping to see a clue to my own schedule. Finally I tire of waiting and return to the hallway. The hallway stretches before and behind me, with a fork going off to the right. They are more like underground tunnels. People walk purposefully in both directions, ignoring me. I feel tired and anxious. I know I have seen my schedule but cannot remember what is on it. A math class, I think, at ten o'clock, but where? I turn over the pages of the math text. It is new, printed on slick, expensive paper, but some pages are already stained. Someone has spilled cooking oil on one page, making a large yellow stain that threatens to soak through to the next pages. Another page is puddled with pancake syrup; the pages might stick together, and I will be unable to learn what is on them.

I begin to think about finding a restroom. I look into one cubicle, but all the fixtures have been removed for remodeling. I look through another doorway, and at the end of a short entryway another door stands ajar revealing what looks like latrine holes in a crumbling stone bench, and shower heads. The latrine has been used and not cleaned. The floor feels spongy under my feet, and I am reluctant to walk on it. Everything looks old, worn, and of questionable cleanliness. I turn away. A few feet away a very tall, naked man stands, black hairs bristling over his whole body, but his facial features are indistinct. The man is holding a towel, evidently wanting to go in to take a shower. I carefully avoid making eye contact or looking at the man's privates and step past him back into the hallway

I think of the previous scenes and of my continuing need to find my class schedule as I drive an automobile on a narrowing road along a low ridge. The campus lies spread out below on my left. The road becomes muddy, then dead-ends at a patch of leafless brush. There is little room to turn around, but I back onto a crumbling shoulder, aware that it might give way at any moment; and it does, causing the automobile to slip backward and downward, stopped by heavy brush. I need to get back to campus to look for my classes. I am aware that the woman in the office is skeptical of my performance so far.

The summer I was twelve years old my parents rented a cabin in pine woods for a week. The air was hot and the smell of the pines was strong. There was a small lake with lily pads and fish. One day I went exploring about the edge of the lake, which was surrounded by pine trees. At the far side of the lake I stepped out of the tree line onto the edge of a field of dried stubble. At the center of the field, about a football field's length away, was a small house. I walked to it, seeing as I neared it that it was old, built of gray, weathered, unpainted wood. There was no glass in the windows, and the door hung on one hinge. I smelled the sun-heated wood. I looked in through a window at what plainly had been the kitchen. The sink and stove had been removed, but there was an old table, and a white granite pan overturned on the floor, and scraps of newspaper. I could see through another door into a room where a metal bed frame sat against the far wall. A piece of red and white checkered oil cloth covered something on the window ledge. I moved the oil cloth aside and saw what I thought was the top of the head of a little goat with nubbins of horns, mounted on a wooden plaque like a trophy. I rubbed the little horns and felt the rough white hair. I pulled the cover back over the little trophy and thought of going inside the house, but I thought it better not to. Years later, as I remember this incident, I think on how unlikely is the part about the goat's head, but I am certain it happened.

That memory returns to me vividly as I climb out of the automobile onto the muddy embankment to consider how to get the automobile back onto the road. The woman from the office stands motionless and silent a few yards from the house, to my left. Her dress clings to the front of her body.

2

Looking down from balcony on second level of shopping mall
Well lighted
Benches

Flashes of gold and green
People moving through
Fluorescent orange underclothing behind plate glass
Dark up here, lights out
Someone behind
Two or three
One dark form in peripheral vision
Rumor in the air:
A shooter in the mall
Moving closer
People continue moving through unconcerned
Should find cover
Try door handle
Unlocked
Dark empty shoe store
Pass between display racks
Door open into lighted room at back
Woman sitting naked on edge of narrow bed with back to door
Turns head slightly to right
"Come in," she says
A drawer slides open at the small of her back
So long since seeing her
A pang of hope
Ask her, "Have you returned to stay?"
"Touch me not," she says
Look into drawer
A revolver
Walking with her on balcony
Hand in hand
Revolver in other hand
"I'm not dressed," she says

"Someone might see me"
She covers her sex with the empty drawer
Why did she say "touch me not"?
Walking together on balcony
Her face is carved wood
Motion to right
Turn quickly pointing revolver
In woods on river bank
She has ascended
Revolver in hand
Motion to right
Cartridges are pencils and sticks

3

The soft flesh of the moon has little in common with the
    slack-faced caricatures
Of minor dictators that appear so often painted on department
    store display windows
The next election might reverse this condition
But for the time being it must be endured
Along with the chains of paper dolls dressed in police uniforms
That festoon all the bridges on the way to City Hall
I, a painter of those caricatures, contemplate that prospect
As I sit with legs dangling over the edge of a bridge
With an arm hooked firmly around a steel girder
But my mind wanders
I would prefer to be painting pictures of a woman I saw as I
    approached the bridge
I saw her only from behind

Dressed in a black sheath with a long zipper down the back
She walked on to the other side of the river
High heels clicking
Hips moving pleasingly beneath the fabric of the dress
Nylon stockings scattering glints of morning sun
Leaving behind her a profusion of musical notation like a cloud of mosquitos
And a faint sweet odor of freshly dry-cleaned police uniforms
I suspect that her unseen face is a tear-gas canister set in a cluster of daffodils
I find this thought arousing
In a few minutes my daily regimen will require me to return to my studio
Necessitating a walk down that long boulevard bordered on both sides by vendors of broken wagon wheels
Fast-food restaurants
Empty lots overgrown with milkweed and marsh grass
I confess to enjoying the pungent odor of the milkweed
Which reminds me of the wife of my youth
Conjurers' supply shops
Opera houses
Museums of erotic toys
A library specializing in works on eighteenth-century Rumanian alchemy
A museum housing a simulation of the surface of the moon
Where children can experience walking on the peculiar sponginess of its flesh
A munitions factory where all the workers are young females cross-trained in the art of Egyptian rug weaving
(Their teeth are recycled piano keys)
A retirement home for disabled poachers

Great heaps of shed puff-adder skins often utilized as wall paper
   for the poor
Or the fabric of costumes for performers in the opera houses
Vendors of antique election campaign buttons
The variety is endless and constantly changing
I find it all tedious
The walk might be somewhat less tedious
If I could anticipate an assignation at the studio with the woman
   in the black dress
But I know in my heart that if I embrace her
Her torso will collapse into an armful of splintered violins
When I arrive at the studio later that morning however
I am consoled by finding a tear gas canister on my doorstep
And a bouquet of daffodils in the pot that holds my paint brushes

4

When I see her next she is standing in the little house
In the field of dried stubble
Her back still turned toward me
Her black sheath dress unzipped
And slipped down off her left shoulder
Exposing the skin of her torso
The drawer has moved up from the small of her back
And is drawn open from her left rib cage
I step through the doorway and approach cautiously
She does not speak or move
In the drawer I see a key
Which I carefully withdraw
Then stand wondering what it will open

And though I do not see her face
I know it is hidden by a white mask
With slits for the eyes and mouth
Through the window beyond her
A procession of children appears from the edge of the woods
And begins to approach slowly
Very slowly, weeks will pass between steps
Hearing the sound of water
I turn to look out the door, holding the key
And see that a spring has begun to flow from beneath the floor
It becomes a stream that carves a channel into the soft earth
    of the field
It soon deepens and I see the many strata of rock beneath
Orange and cream and black and red
The smell of hot stone under the noon sun permeates the air
As the river rushes downward through the canyon
Toward the warm salt sea that lies with its knees raised
    in the abyss below
Waiting to be healed
And I reach up and insert the key into the sun

Wall attempts to cover its breasts

Wall attempts to cover its breasts with songs of breaking glass
Man in Stetson puts head through noose and grins
Tiny fragments of glass shower him with praise
"Let some words be yours alone," he says
Wall folds, hides in corner with unendurable shame
Head falls off man in Stetson
Stetson's crown is breast of wall
"Hoard them, treasure them"

Ars Poetica

1

The gift of language presents itself
In a night that lives beneath layers of rock
Words pick their way through slowly
Be patient

2

Let go of the handful of ropes
The ships full sail will glide away backward
Their destinations written on a motel room wall
Where a man sits alone on the edge of the bed with a clear stone in his hand
Hoping to translate them

3

Watch for words to rise from a well,
Bright, clear.
Snatch them, one by one.

4

A burgundy Porsche (it is warm chocolate)

Wraps itself mindlessly around a lamppost
Incites it to flash neon poems.
This occurs with some frequency in the gardens of temples
That hide in the depths of canyons,
In shadows,
Behind boulders,
Beside springs around which deer and lions and many
    smaller creatures
Congregate to consider the meaning of what is etched on the walls.
The woman who walks the canyons
(Sometimes she is old, sometimes she is young;
Sometimes she is naked, sometimes she is clothed)
Sometimes pauses to interpret,
But the animals never think to write her words
(It could be done with a tip of an antler or a claw
And a small offering of blood).
It is rumored that they are written on light
Behind the pages of old books,
And sometimes the pages are thin enough to reveal them.
They may also be enciphered by flashing streetlamps
And the drippings of melting Porsches.

5

Yesterday a stone spoke of dried-up seas and stunted grass
In obedience to rules of prosody laid down by trout that flash
    in sunlight
They remember solemnly the girls who dance in woods
The girls' eyes are large and wide.
They are not fooled by foolish men who lose their shoes when
    passing through a room,

Who cling by the fingernails to the surface of the smooth sphere
   that rises from the lake
From beneath the roots of water lilies afloat in the night
"Forget me not," the night says as it slips behind the moon to rest
   and heal.
Its wounds gape and are very painful.
It is wounded mysteriously every time it walks in the empty streets
Where battle tanks and kelp groves once reigned over a populace of
   poets and metaphysicians
Who scratched futilely at the faces of tall buildings trying
   to catch hold.

6

A raven said:
Unto what shall I liken these mysteries,
   that you may understand?
Behold, who has seen them has seen rain fly up from the earth;
   behold, he has seen it;
Nevertheless, the stones creep beneath the garden,
   forgetful of rain and violets;
The violets peer about expectantly,
   but the stones forget to embrace them.
Even so, rain flies up from the earth;
   iron butterflies cavort in sunshine;
Therefore shall the violets remember
   that they have seen fire, have seen rain;
That the river of lies that flows down from that lost star,
   that runs beneath the balconies of a spacious building—
The dreams that stumble into it can remember yet their innocence;

otherwise, the violets must forsake all hope of marriage.
Behold, may these things not be likened
   unto the sayings of that woman who lives in deep woods,
She who is sometimes old, sometimes young,
   who sometimes goes clothed, sometimes naked?
She sends out dreams to twelve dreamers—
   to one a white rabbit;
   to another an ambassadress of saltpeter;
   to another an iron butterfly;
And so on unto all the twelve,
   unto each in his time,
Unto each according to the word that comes to her
   from the night that lives behind rock.
Each inscribes his dream in the patina of a canyon wall;
   each ponders his inscription;
Each reaches forth to touch the fire that lives behind it,
   behind the rock, behind the night where stones lie with violets.

7

Touch a word and a whole language trembles in anticipation
The couple in the cherry tree lips and tongues

Portrait of the Artist as a Young Man

A young man, a promising poet, sits on the edge of a bunk in a civilian internment camp, clutching a crystal sphere, his eyes stopped blinking, open. The walls of the barrack are covered with tarpaper, and bare lightbulbs hang from the ceiling on black insulated wiring. The young man is shirtless and his skin is pale. He has just showered (this camp is regularly inspected by the Red Cross and is known for its sanitary conditions) and his skin smells clean. Someone goes outside to tell a guard, and two internees are ordered to carry the body out and put it in a wheelbarrow and take it to a ditch that has been freshly dug at the edge of the camp just inside the chain link fence and dump it in. Guards throw dice for the crystal sphere, which is later reported resting on top of the ethyl pump at an abandoned service station in Arizona.

"Your poems are querulous"

"Your poems are querulous."
So says the woman who leaves the table,
Frowning with disapproval.
Querulous? But she may be right,
And I would prefer to hide in a huckleberry bush,
Feet in the roots, hands extended into the leaves.

A PARABOLA SUPINE ON THE FLOOR

A parabola supine on the floor
Imitates cries of sea gulls lost in the sun
Scraps of paper blowing across a desert cry as well but in
    higher register
The parabola undulates on the swells of the Pacific

"Help me," you say

"Help me," you say.
"I can't reach the drawer under my left shoulder blade."
You sit on the edge of a bed,
Flesh glowing in morning light.
I stand on the floor beside you,
Open the drawer,
And see a needle, a thimble, a pigeon feather, a tiny mirror, a flowering pear tree,
A slowly moving stream with banks covered by sun-warmed grass,
A miniature oil painting depicting the beheading of a false shaman,
A black seed spat out by Eve.
"I want a pear blossom," you say,
And I pluck one and place it on your left thigh.
Later, emerging from sleep,
I catch a glimpse of a black seed floating away on the stream.

A grand piano on a pier

A grand piano on a pier against a sunset
Plays a fugue slowly
Dice of teeth rattle in a cup
Fall on the pier
In a pattern predicted by equations written in the treble clef
A dwarf in yellow huddled against a piano leg
Picks up the tune in perfect falsetto
The sun after setting shines from his throat

Sixteen small stones

Sixteen small stones, white and smooth
Sixteen stones engraved with an image of the sun
Sixteen girls with stone eyes guard the door of the temple
Sixteen songs coil about temple pillars
Sixteen dwarves with daffodil feet dance on the sea bottom
Sixteen unicorns twist their horns into insoluble knots
Sixteen ships bombard the custom house of regret
Sixteen fish whirl ecstatically in fire
Sixteen faded memories drip from the ceiling
Sixteen portraits hang beneath a bridge
Sixteen wrecked bridges hold an army at a river
Sixteen lost wars petition for reinstatement
Sixteen brides nail themselves to elevator walls
Sixteen coins mistake themselves for poems
Sixteen islands offer asylum to unsuccessful lies
Sixteen lies wait in darkness for lovers

Silent meditations on torn lingerie

Silent meditations on torn lingerie glisten in summer sun
On wharves of gilt lilies and egg yokes shorn of dogs
Of hairy giraffes burning
Burning on hills of life
In desert
In city
Empty streets melt in glare of mushroom clouds
Let us go down
Let us go down
Let us go down to the sea again
In ships dragged through empty streets
Melting streets
Gutters of pure gold
Sketched on thighs of sad streetwalkers
They have sad eyes
They have red ribbons in their hair
Torn ribbons

Your Eyes Wide Behind Mine

Your eyes wide behind mine,
Surprised after long search
Among boulders,
Through canyons,
To come upon such a view.
We somersault backward,
Above tips of fir trees,
Forest beneath us stretching over the horizon.
Rumors pass of an ocean beyond.

Beneath Littered Streets Persist Rumors of Ill Will

Beneath littered streets persist rumors of ill will
Toward royal personages who mutter under their breath.
Fourteen varieties of genetically engineered strawberry vines dangle
    from their teeth.
I would be troubled were the sun to splinter against a betrayal,
But meanwhile I take comfort in bark detaching from
    dead aspens—
The fibrous inner side makes a wonderful tinder.

A battle tank laden with violets

A battle tank laden with violets, roots and all, bursts from
     the pavement,
Hunches its shoulders, on each of which perches a little man
Holding a portrait of Dear Leader.
The curb's eyes look up wide with wonder and fear.
The tank proceeds with self-assurance
Between tall buildings with black façades.
They have many windows with white sills.
Ghosts of dreams of memories of courage rush about hysterically,
Mindless of the futility of hopes to escape
Into the depths of a lake among stems of water lilies.
Better to hide behind a portrait of Dear Leader.
The tank moves on past the edge of the city, to the beach, toward
     the sea.
It disintegrates into sand.

Axels roll and clang down a desert highway

Axels roll and clang down a desert highway,
Trade amongst themselves stories of loves lost in canyons of desire,
Where the drivers of dairy trucks shave their legs before prayer
And remember ancient days
When a beam of sunlight reflected from a rabbit skull
Could find sanctuary in a forgotten book.
These stories slip from a lover's fingertips
And inscribe themselves in blue ink on the skin of a beloved,
On the skin along the spine.

Let both thy legs be spinning tops

Let both thy legs be spinning tops.
A window pane that cuts us in half
Would find more satisfaction in cotton threads
Hung from a clothesline across the abyss of desire.
The sides are sandstone cliffs red in noonday sun.
White rabbits browse in the crevices.
At the bottom of the canyon a caravan of Buicks,
Glass flashing, roofs hot,
Picks its way carefully among boulders.
We park at the canyon's edge,
The road narrowing, turning downward
Under pine trees, blocked by boulders.
We see through the windshield over the edge
The caravan of Buicks picking its way.
Both thy legs are spinning tops.

Against black a torso

Against black a torso
Beside it a cluster of crystals
Grasp the crystals
Edges and points
Clear, sapphire
In the depth of crystal your eyes
Open, unblinking

Suspended in space

Suspended in space
Spread-eagled face to face
Our hands nailed
Our feet nailed
Our breath mingled
The suns in our loins fused

Textbook solutions always leak

Textbook solutions always leak:
Sand in a child's pail finds its way to the sea;
The vertex of a parabola opens to a troupe of clowns.
These are consequences of an oft-ignored axiom:
Pharà ba ten ma na tian,
Malikna ba ten sa ánia.

This rose unfolding its petals

This rose unfolding its petals
Must be enjoyed discreetly
To avoid inciting revolution
Among software designers in white shirts
Who wait at train stations in the early hours of desire
When the Word flows down the faces of tall buildings like
    dripping paint,
For the alternative surely is chaos:
Brass bands and clowns invading Sunday meetings
As conducting officers throw up their hands to declare,
"I surrender to joy!"
As newly-weds explore the *Kama Sutra* in temple gardens.

Melchizedek and his bride

Melchizedek and his bride roll with abandon in grass.
Words once lost swarm from every blade.

A SPIRIT RISES FROM OUR BED

A spirit rises from our bed,
Withholds its hand,
Its head a seer stone:
See the flower garden
Bright in sunlight.
You offer an azalea,
A snap dragon, a tiger lily.
We stand on a bridge that disintegrates,
A cloud of butterflies.
We fly with them.

Is not Babylon a golden cup in the Lord's hand?

Is not Babylon a golden cup in the Lord's hand?
It collects light;
A woman dances in it;
Veils whirl about her,
Brush the waxed finish of a new automobile,
Red and gleaming,
All in harmony with the owner's manual for the universe
Kept secure in a box
At the center of the Crab Nebula,
Or if not there, surely elsewhere—
No one has ever doubted it.

A rainbow straightens; it is a flower stem

A rainbow straightens; it is a flower stem.
Be careful—the box in which it is stored
Is a treacherous cat that has walked on the water of desire
That puddles seductively on the settee in the operating room
Where children examine through crystalizing eyes
A book illustrated with colored plates
Of the atrocities committed in Nanking.
They are explicit as a handful of rabbits' teeth on an unmade bed.
The rainbow knows but is secure in its box,
Observing dispassionately through a bedroom window
The maneuvers on a hillside of a squadron of toy automobiles
Training for the next war.
It will begin in August (not this August)
And flow down the ravine, down from the hill,
A river of tiny wheels and crystalized eyes.

Daneel Olivaw and André Breton are rafting to Tahiti

Daneel Olivaw and André Breton are rafting to Tahiti.
They invite Enoch,
Who is detained by a late vision
But promises to join them for a game of gō
And lends them a seer stone found in a nest of Easter eggs,
Pastel blue and yellow,
Like these flowers floating about our bedroom.
They orbit around the clock, a wind-up.
The yellow ones talk with the seer stone in anxious whispers.
It says there could be lunch with Gauguin,
But he is annoyed by false ticks of the clock.
They are dried kisses dropping one per second onto his
    wet canvases.
The clock itself sits ignored on a corner of the raft.
Raindrops blue and yellow freckle the face of that brown girl who
    counts them.
They are the true ticks of the clock.
Poets know this,
And brown girls
Whose breasts project wiring diagrams onto the walls
    of Gauguin's hut.

You unlock yourself

You unlock yourself
And swing back the door between your ribs and your navel
To allow the golden wire coils of a symphony of insurrection
To spill forth across both sides of the bed onto the floor
Through the door into the kitchen to liquefy
It is water two inches deep
I attempt to squeegee it together
To hold it against a wall away from the stove
Where a large kettle of broth is coming to a boil
Light reflected from the coils flashing on the walls and ceiling
For an instant we are a full-grown cherry tree heavy with fruit bursting from the ground
I help you collect the coils in handfuls and stuff them back into the darkness
And you push me inside and close the door and lock it

Proverbs

The swift polarity of prying eyes like sin waiting at the door
eats cherries through the wanton nights of used car lots
   under duress.
A hand beneath a blouse seeks trails through constellations
   of doubt
that rotate on ordinates of intercalated wantonness.
The ionized kisses of a mistress of antiquated wars are not
   more beautiful
than a bouquet of doubts on a windowsill on the morning of
   an execution.
A windowsill undulating between two colors of a rainbow
is the analog of hammer blows in the interstices of a
   rattlesnake's vertebrae.
The undulations of the Andromeda Galaxy are sweet as a
   rattlesnake's eyes,
but the loves of used car lots pierce like an antiquated war's tooth.

THE URIM OF A JEWELRY BOX WHISPERS ENDEARMENTS

The urim of a jewelry box whispers endearments to the thummim of a suspension bridge in the throes of temporary dismemberment,
As hanging in air over a rising river of piano notes in high register they wonder together at five things:
The way of a lark's tongue with seven-cornered dice,
A promising kiss from Sacagawea contorting in a secret compartment of Meriwether Lewis's spy glass,
A flash of cannon fire held in secret and reluctant reserve from the Mexican War,
A way of looking at a blackbird dismissed by establishment critics as the final belated cowardice of a maimed gun-runner
But recognized by frequenters of reptile zoos on Route 66 as a stroke of pure intelligence from beyond the night where stones and violets exchange caresses.
Then beyond the penultimate ridge a final crescendo of piano notes tumbling up the face of a heaving talus slide of cartridges full metal jacket specially engineered for full automatic fire
And finding in the press of one more key apotheosis in a backward somersault by the jewelry box and the suspension bridge into the violet-colored stars at the center of the galaxy

Rain falls through the night

Rain falls through the night,
Sleep hiding,
Maybe under the stage where the sins of my youth prance and leer.
When it returns, we will lie side by side and talk
Of the time when I and the girl were naked and I was a boy,
When we talked with the rabbits and the deer,
Before she began to talk with the snake.

In the place where rain flies upward from the earth

In the place where rain flies upward from the earth,
Girls weave grass and random threads of night.
They make baskets for the collection of buttons
That spring in full blossom from idle conversation;
Girls who stand half revealed in doorways of long halls.
They beckon with hands of four fingers.
They live in glass houses of lavender tint;
Equations etched on the walls trail over the windowsills.
The nipples of the equations gaze brazenly out from
    between parentheses.
The aureoles are in watercolor.
To make baskets with four-fingered hands is a rare talent.
The patterns woven into the baskets are revealed by shamanic hares
Who share the girls' beds through long nights of computation.
The resultant equations trail over the windowsills,
Enlace themselves in patterns of equivocal time spread across
    the grounds,
Down to the edge of the great lake on which a white house has
    been built not far from shore.
Its windows are lavender.
Through a lower window a girl looks out, offering a bouquet
    of buttons.
She speaks equations.
Her lips move unheard from this distance.

BEHIND A WATERFALL
AN ABANDONED SERVICE STATION

Behind a waterfall an abandoned service station decays under
 Arizona sun
On Route 66 of an old man's desire
As the pages of a Louis L'Amour paperback turn yellow and brittle.
Read it while sitting on a rock beside the highway—
The robot army that flows over a distant ridge
Will divide and pass harmlessly on both sides around you
(The robot soldiers dream of sleep on beds of dew-damp violets).
You can read this promise in a note hidden in a coffee can by
 Jubal Sackett.
It was guarded faithfully for years by a girl in a light summer dress
Whose brain lies in precisely divided sections on the service
 station counter.
She hid the note in a concrete wigwam until the wigwam was
 commandeered by a robot officer
During the war with a cousin of Gadianton who threatened the
 visible desert
With a visible flood of visible treacherous memories of a kiss,
Before the girl's brain surrendered to inevitable dissection near the
 ethyl pump.
(If this is cryptic, look for the solution stored in glyphs in the
 fragments of a broken crystal sphere.)
In the run-up to the war, she served as a spy for the robot army,
Was known for her magical tongue that had licked every line of
 every glyph,

Encoding it with the coordinates of every waterfall behind which old men hide.

The hour is nigh and the day soon at hand

The hour is nigh and the day soon at hand
When the ambassador of the moon's blood
Turns the key to open that museum
Where the heads of the apostate kings are displayed.
It will be on a clear glass night freshly blown,
When the sun's hearse arrives early at the concert hall.
That is the first sign. The second sign
Is the sudden evaporation of the official musicians
Under the very eyes of a visiting trumpeter,
The one who leads the little dog
By a leash of false prophecies—
The musicians think themselves clever to disguise themselves
In the clothes made of the trumpeter's nose hairs;
Or so it has been thought by soldiers whose eyes
Falling from their sockets roll and rattle
Together down the streets where a cheering crowd
Has gathered all night for a victory parade.
"And I will burn them up," saith the ambassador,
"In a bonfire of self-recognition."

The first time I saw rain through an Edward Hopper painting

The first time I saw rain through an Edward Hopper painting was a Christmas when the two sparrows of my greatest regret were dragged down the highway by a moving van driven by the last shot fired in the war between the sphinxes. Their bones protrude from the sand like Japanese fans planted in the desert of our discontent. Few of us are content with the fruit that derives from the dynamite forest, our legs protruding from under the bed serving as question marks on a billboard of desire that paints your forehead with tiny figures of Gandy dancers in slow motion. (None of this has ever found its way into a Hopper painting.)

The reason I stole shoes
from the legs of an easel in the MOMA

The reason I stole shoes from the legs of an easel in the MOMA was that rain was crawling across the floor with four dog hairs in its teeth. I had never done that before, except in the case of extreme degradation by pots of boiling broth distributed to vagrant mannequins in the last workshop of radiant hypocrisy. My guilt is an Egyptian barge carrying poems and the raisins preferred by dogs underneath the Nile all the way to the split infinitives at the top of the dial. This is not to be explained to children whose eyes form the center line of a highway.

This is no accident

This is no accident.
Its roots extend past that Kuiper Belt of consciousness
Where on the shaded porch of an overlooked house
Three abstract daughters of a half-conjugated verb
Leap from an airship of obsolete wars.
This is according to a musical score delivered by a rabbit on the eve of love,
When gravel flung across a highway agitates for change.
Let us be less dismissive of reports from the front
Transmitted telepathically by rows of sparrows
Sitting on telephone lines.
Their minds are green
But good for carrying groceries
Across miles and miles of barren waste.
This is the wish of the three daughters.
They lay themselves down on a strip of aluminum siding
Feet to head, feet to head.
They meditate on transcriptions of sleeping stories
Whispered from the upper thigh of one of them,
Though she is shy to admit it.

And God called the light Day

And God called the light Day,
And the darkness he called Night.
So very simple,
More so than the radiance of boats that leave their slippers
    by the fireside
When they glimmer away,
Moths bedazzled by visions of deer in great troupes
That scratch at the brick fronts of dissolving buildings hoping
    for remission
Of the residual guilt of grass in the twilight of a kiss.
The grass parts before our liquid steps
As a ray of pure intelligence from Alpha Centauri B
(Though its existence is questioned)
Is refracted through a dewdrop
That divides itself by zero.

Speaking of old books

Speaking of old books,
There is one on the third shelf down,
Third from the left,
On the Showman's Trail,
A secret compartment cut into the pages.
It holds a cedar-wood box.
In the box is the palace
Of the Little Lame Prince.
At the highest level of the southwestern tower
Is a room where a fire is kept,
Though the room is rarely visited.
Under a vase on a small black table,
In an envelope sealed with red wax,
Is a Christmas card
Depicting a sleigh ride,
A village steeple,
Silver glitterdust for falling snow,
As I am clasped by your legs
In zero gravity

THE OLD WOMAN WHO LIVES IN DEEP WOODS

The old woman who lives in deep woods
Is aware of developments in the capital,
For news travels fast through the root systems,
A fact often overlooked in the histories
That generations of urban spiders have woven into their webs;
But her eyes are the dewdrops on the filaments.

In the No Thing from which all things rise

In the No Thing from which all things rise,
Trees, when they make love,
Conjugate the orbit of the square root of a thigh.

The skin of a telephone pole

The skin of a telephone pole has the texture of cardboard boxes out of tune,
Each one sounding the alarm to warn the birds that say no,
The big ones that hang from a chain stretched between towns,
In one of which survives a small independent movie theater
Where school children pry out their teeth with scissors,
Leaving each pair when they are finished impaled upright on the top of a fencepost,
A fence across southwest Oregon to keep out itinerant dreams
Of a woman who offers a mango seed
Flat in her palm as a piano keyboard stretching to the horizon.
"The car won't start," the woman says.
It is parked on the shoulder of a road in the country where worn-out love is stacked like tires behind service stations.
Then climbing in the superstructure of a bridge made of balsa wood sticks,
Carefully guarding a clear stone in my pocket,
I remember that I am already late for morning formation.
There will be a court martial.
I will present as my defense the black keys of the mango seed,
But I know that the defense of Oregon is already
    fatally compromised,
And I regret this as the eye of a needle regrets the passage of escaping motor oil.

The table is set in the banquet hall

The table is set in the banquet hall:
White napkins, crystal, and flowers;
At each place a fading photograph of a war bride.
The walls are red and hung with oil paintings.
At the end of the hall a child plays on the floor,
A girl in a white dress.
A net of quivering language drops from the ceiling
But remains hovering above her.
The sound of one piano note could release it.

A FLOCK OF STARLINGS COLLAPSING SUDDENLY TO A PERIOD

A flock of starlings collapsing suddenly to a period suspended against the sky
Is reminiscent of the membrane that connects the whisperings of lovers to the engines of eighteen-wheel trucks
That speed through the mirror-walled labyrinth called history.
The black point marks the boundary between the memory of a first kiss accompanied by a first laying of bare hands on a bare back
And the meditations of mannequins abandoned on a beach.
One of them, suspicious of the others, concentrates on the image of a snake coiled in sunshine on a compost heap.
When you approach them they all assume the aspect of new flowers in a garden of suspect conjugations.
You yourself can escape suspicion by concentrating on meadows, rabbits, red-tiled rooves, thin-gloved hands, leaps of logic, leaping salmon, centipedes, mice, empty soup cans, tunnels of abandoned uranium mines in southern Utah, the vanishing of a river into sand, any horn of any of Daniel's beasts, the typography of the text that veils the faces of all the ones that you have loved.

Here is the secret exit
from the theater of the mind

Here is the secret exit from the theater of the mind that floats on a black river.
Sometimes it stands in glaring sunlight on the red earth of a street in a Brazilian village—
The theater, that is.
It is the last refuge of young brides who emerge in pairs from the splitting bark of pine trees.
If you lie for several hours supine on the street in the later afternoon with your eyes fixed on the equations unfurling in the upper atmosphere,
The girl in the ticket booth will come and lift you by the hand
And give you answer to your prayers concerning the source and the destination of the black river,
Where it empties into the warm sea of flowers and memories red with old hesitation.
The interior of the theater is cool and dark.
The box seats are especially well positioned for viewing assassinations in real time.

A MAN IN ORANGE COVERALLS AND SAFETY GOGGLES

A man in orange coveralls and safety goggles climbing carefully down a ladder inside an enormous concrete vat of boiling water lets go of the ladder and without a sound or motion signifying alarm or pain slips into the water and floats face up. After the body is recovered in a complex and lengthy operation involving chains and grappling hooks it is determined by a forensic team flown in by the FBI at the request of the local police chief that the man probably is dead before he hits the water. A few days later it is reported by a local television station that the chief has for several years carried on an affair with the man's wife, who since early adolescence has been obsessed by a secret fetish for having the backs of her thighs caressed with fresh flowers. There is no evidence, however, of any complicity by either the chief or the wife in the man's death, and no charges are ever brought against them. Curiously, the media never address the question, what is the purpose of the vat of boiling water? And that despite the fact that runoff from the vat has for years irrigated lush and brilliant fields of tulips on the rooftops of Los Angeles office buildings. When the wife is asked about this use of the water as she is interviewed by a reporter while walking naked through a tunnel of mirrors beneath the city, dragging her finger tips lightly along the surface of the glass, she refers the reporter to the appendix of an exhaustive report on the cultivation of tulips, the only known copy of which is classified "Top Secret—POTUS Eyes Only" (everyone involved in its preparation having been subjected to a memory wipe) and kept in a vault in the Oval Office with another blue dress. The case then disappears entirely from the news.

Sitting in a camp chair in a patch of alders

Sitting in a camp chair in a patch of alders trying to ignore the eyes that watch from a leaf.
Seeds pour steadily from a rift in the sky.
Each has an eye.
The situation is alarming,
And the clock on the tower of the municipal building adjacent to the alder patch speaks in tongues.
For those who can interpret, it reports without judgment the loves of seafarers from the next county,
Or the next century.
The solution to the puzzle is written on the sails of small ships rotting with skepticism.

The lake's nipples quiver under the gaze of a receding paragraph

The lake's nipples quiver under the gaze of a receding paragraph.
The embarrassment of the trees is palpable.
The sun bleeds out on a carpet of desire.
Paper cups will scoop up the residue
And spread it on a table built of fresh disappointment.
Look for the map drawn on the surface of the lake.
Touch it—it vibrates.
Its continents are mist sucked back into a bottle.
Its mountains are the eyes of a feral cat
Surprised in the act of love with a bunch of crabgrass.
Its oceans are named *in absentia.*
Its meridians are snipped by scissors,
The scissor blades that are long-stemmed flowers
That kneel on the map table of prayer.

At the horizon line of my woman's shoulder

At the horizon line of my woman's shoulder,
a tank regiment pauses to reconnoiter.
The tanks are very small,
but as dangerous as wire threaded from the tip of a snake's tail to the tips of its tongue.
I pick my way toward my woman through webs of tripwires.
They reflect the light of half-memories
of a red button at rest on the tip of my tongue,
of flowers picked in the garden where the teardrops of a forgotten war hide from the spies of the morning,
where the prisoners that survive vivisection in the interrogation tents of hope lie in wait,
hidden in discarded seed packages,
in the garden where memory is a pair of scissors that snips a battle plan at its root.

A CONTINGENT OF UNDEFINED PAIN STAGES AN INCIDENT ON THE BORDER

A contingent of undefined pain stages an incident on the border between sorrow and an alarm clock.
This is an attempt to provoke a war, but if hostilities break out you can hide behind any numeral of the clock.
You will notice that the clock is growing feathers—you may pluck it bare as time's thigh tattooed with a map out of this hotel where disaffected syntax watches from inside the bed posts.
It is prudent, however, not to notice that time darts through the hallway and around the corner to hide from the sheriff with grotesquely thick legs who searches for it here every night.
Avoid touching his legs—beneath his trousers they are bundles of feathers with many mouths that will attempt to suck you in to the holding tank of the clock's unclaimed ticks.
Eventually the night clerk, who is a woman of a certain age, will come around with the number of the feathers.
It is said to be the security code for the lock on the exit door, if you understand the dialect in which she speaks it.
If you attempt to copulate with her, you will find that she wears always one more layer of clothing.

I cannot find your kisses on this map

I cannot find your kisses on this map,
And the roof is made of flower stems.
It will not last the night
Of rain so bright it cannot be described mathematically.
Other lovers quarrel in the street.
Their clothes hang from the arch of a bridge
Against a backdrop of complex plumbing
From which starlings flow upward.
I would hold your shoulders and kiss you while hiding
    among the starlings,
But I cannot find your kisses on this map.

Fleeing the scene

FLEEING THE SCENE
FLEEING RESPONSIBILITY
FLEEING THE INTERVIEW
There is a good deal of fleeing, a young woman points out,
One who is skilled at vaginal contraction,
Eve learned of that skill from the white hare that prayed through the spider's web.
It spoke with her at length as the waters receded gradually toward the edges of the earth.
These thoughts revolve with the planets as one passes through the city square.
These buildings—they will wash away when the floods return.
The secrets that hide in them fork on an endless decision tree.
One thinks of settling comfortably into the driver's seat of a red convertible
And driving leisurely through southern California,
Through the stratified fissure that opens in Ginsberg's best lines,
Sandstone orange, sandstone red, sandstone black,
Smelling hot in the sunlight.
It leads to a beach, where, standing in the sand in highly polished shoes,
One remembers the smell of a freshly washed and ironed blue dress
That descends over a young woman's freshly washed body
As gently, as quietly, as smoothly as a robin's egg descends into the gullet of a snake.

A salal leaf grows from my palm

A salal leaf grows from my palm
It does not compute interest
As a canoe emerges from the leaf
Looks about
Sees that traffic is heavy on the freeway
Going softly
It parts the salal bushes on the median strip
Going softly
Salal growing on the stairs
A dust cloud pervades the imagination
Fishhooks dangled in the ivy
And why must I wait so long for a kiss from the woman who lives
   in the woodshed?
She smiles from a block of wood
A river slips silently and unobtrusively from beneath the woodpile
Creeps under the door and bolts for the sea
Carrying her smile in its pocket
The smile is very knowing
It has lived where the songs emerge whole from loaves of bread
What its fingers have touched is the first secret that lives beneath
   the stairs
The salal bushes are deeply rooted in it
The canoe sits high on the water
A quantum of salal leaves is very light
A quantum of reminiscence flits in and out of existence
Now it sits on the prow of the canoe
Now it slides down the arm

The smile is very knowing
The balustrade creeps down the slope toward the river
White, it fails to attain its objective
The further end lies in fragments
The fingers have touched them
The fingers know that the hand cannot grasp itself
The quantum of reminiscence progresses along the sleeve

I RECEIVE A LETTER FROM A WOMAN PROMISING LOVE AT AN UNSPECIFIED DATE

I receive a letter from a woman promising love at an
 unspecified date.
It evokes a constellation of memories—
The warm water of the river that flows from beneath a small house
 just outside the edge of a pine forest;
A fold of silk;
A heap of rose petals in my cupped hand,
In each an eye that has seen the dawn
Where songs hide curled like four-week fetuses in the corners
 beneath stairways.
The late President clutches with bloody hands at the stiletto in the
 base of his throat.
I am nearly overcome by drowsiness as I read.
Her name is Legion, and the edges of her shadow are feathered.
Resolving to ignore the drowsiness, I walk out into the street,
Which as I walk becomes a canyon of Wingate sandstone
Where water is scarce but can be found trickling from faucets at
 approximately shoulder height.
I recognize the contours of her belly in the sandstone adjacent to
 one of the faucets
And take refuge from the sun by sitting in the shade within
 her navel.
Her letter is tattooed on my back.

Your breasts are bird's eggs

Your breasts are bird's eggs, smooth but not speckled
Sleeping curled on your left aureole
I dream of the afternoon when we are glyphs etched in
    desert patina
The sun is high but we are on the southern wall of a canyon and
    the sun never touches us
After your breasts hatch I will keep the broken shells in a basket
    woven of your eyelashes

The woman in the street huddles under her wings

The woman in the street huddles under her wings
She is ignored by passers-by, who are preoccupied by the moths that flutter in the hollows of their silhouettes
She grieves for the legless children who hide behind the false building fronts that have been set up along the street by anonymous volunteers for the benefit of tourists
The tourist industry in this country predates by many years the publication of Boileau's *Art Poétique*
But be careful of the ants—they have friends in high places where the historical archives are burned for heat in winter
Winter comes unexpectedly in this country close behind the elk herds that step hesitantly out from between the false fronts like rancid guilt
When I was a legless child hiding behind a false front I sometimes looked up from scriptural texts to see the herds step out from beyond the horizon

A PERIOD WORKING ITS WAY DOWN THE TUBE OF A THERMOMETER

A period working its way down the tube of a thermometer pauses for conversation with the birds of late desire
I have no idea where it has laid the axel discarded by the moving van of regret
I pat its down-covered belly with an ivory drumstick
It purrs like a cat whose legs are borrowed from a dinner table
Stare at the period long enough and all six of its wings unfurl into a winter of harpsichord notes

"Ye were also—in the beginning"

"Ye were also—in the beginning"
The words excreted in the sap of an alder tree
I lay myself under it to sleep and dream
Of secure employment as an implementation software designer
And wake to the reality of a river of elk antlers
Flowing from beneath the roots

Always the first time?

Always the first time?
A handful of grapes
The little fox whose teeth are box cutters
Leads the procession out from the shade and the cool of the mission church
Into the bright sunlight of apocryphal polemics
A soap dish could demolish the argument
Always the first time
I place a peeled grape between your teeth

Small snake coiled

Small snake coiled
In drawer of a dressing table
Built of red cedar
(Fragrant)
In corner of lady's private chamber
She is the one whose head is a glittering fountain
Or a sedge of bitterns
(It is said to depend on the position of Saturn relative to Orion)
She was one's lover once
Before the stream that issues from beneath the cottage
Divided into four and evaporated
Into glittering confetti
Reflecting a face on every flake
It is familiar
It was once the lady's

An eye in each fingertip

An eye in each fingertip
Lingering doubts about the efficacy of certain prayers
Looking out from the center of a crystal sphere
The stairway festooned with yellow flowers
A brief kiss on lips
A walk in the garden
The eyes of your fingertips blink rapidly

WALKING IN A GARDEN
WE SEE IN THE DISTANCE CLOCKS

Walking in a garden we see in the distance clocks hanging in the arches of a bridge
Your white hand rests palm up
We have made love under that bridge
The memory of it is a cloud of dragonflies rising up from the hand

Arrican France, for a time

Arrican France, for a time
Splitting a mullein fruit with a thumbnail
At the moment when pleasure is incandescent pain
A heavy serpent descends between hills
Scales glisten in the sunlight
Arrican is the word that fills its mind
See its eye that is a clock
From where do such words come?
A mullein fruit holds many seeds
Incandescence is a swan that opens its breast with two hands
France is a clock

Driving a blue convertible on a country road

Driving a blue convertible on a country road in sunshine, this girl's head resting on my shoulder: her head white and shaped like something made of rubber, but her breasts firm and gleaming in the sunlight, her dress with a floral pattern (the front of the dress being cut away to expose her chest and upper abdomen) smells freshly washed and ironed. Then we are climbing together in the cables of a suspension bridge; the cables also gleaming in the sunlight. From this vantage we look on busy streets painted with unknown letters, but we recognize the word. Will she go away if I attempt to kiss her? But the rubber thing that is her head has no lips.

The prairie grass in my heart

The prairie grass in my heart is silent as a broken pane of glass
And sleep remains elusive: it spills from my hands, dry
   and crumbling

In the grass-infested cylinders of a Model T engine

Intimation of despair in the grass-infested cylinders of a Model T
 engine set on sawhorses under walnut trees
The grass dry as the memory of virginity in a cluttered warehouse
 of remorse
The oil pooled on the ground of being looks about warily
Beware the rainbow sheen it is a map
And the warehouse is marked in blue
And is not trustworthy

Remorse is a decaying house on the outskirts of town

Remorse is a decaying house on the outskirts of town
Beyond are fields where the grass is uncut and dry
The woman who looks out the window has binoculars
She is a magpie
She is the fragrance of a hand of playing cards jack of diamonds
Her thoughts are a curve in a stairway
Her thoughts are the curve of an elliptical seerstone
We loved her once
Wind sways the grass
The flight of a magpie persists

I attach great importance to life

I attach great importance to life
Standing here on this threshold of
The door that opens in two directions
Standing here on the edge of
A watermelon seed
On a sunlit street on a strip of beach
Girls in bathing suits water droplets on their skin
    refracting sunlight
Where it makes perfect sense to say that ninety percent of the
    instances of HIV occurring in the shells of pigeons' eggs are
    attributable to the absence of orange Kool-Aid in the pudenda
    of boxcars, the ones that have painted on their outer surfaces the
    remnants of alphabets lost for centuries, as Sherpa guides
    meditate on the peels of oranges apples bananas all manner of
    goat and numerous species of vascular plant
Where a word turns on its axis
Where a word's color becomes another
"No, I Don't Think So."
"No, I don't think so."
"But why, if the corner of the door is curling like the corner of a
    sheet of white paper?"
"That's just what they said. The smoke curls above the roofs."
"Then it won't be today."
But it is the smoke, after all
As we stroll on the beach
The buttons under our feet are so deep and slippery

This mixture of invective and possibility appears on the terrorist
    watch list
It spills, black sand, off both sides of my palm

Curl of a Hand

Curl of a hand
Curl of a leaf
Curl of a petal
Curve of a feather
The feather lies on the highway
It is regulated by an agency that lives under the skin of the head
Fishhooks attach themselves to the head
Their leaders radiate outward by static electricity
The petal is the skirt of an emaciated girl
She is a forgotten daughter of a Fisher King
Who wraps his limbs around the trunk of a pine tree
As tall as the ceiling of a drunkard's kitchen
I sleep with a petal over each eye
They are translucent and very suggestive

Open the abdomen of the sun

Open the abdomen of the sun
Its entrails spill onto the beach
The fish heads of ignominy are painted on the walls—blue streaks
We should leave in the morning—there will be anger under
    the stairs
I think the crack in the window glass is an *ad hominem* argument
And the cracks in the pavement have gone fishing with a flock
    of sparrows
I sit on the edge of a bed with my eyes closed
My eyes are closed and my shoulders sag forward
My eyes are closed and my hands dangle between my knees
I smell smoke
I smell a buffalo
I smell a rattlesnake
I smell the skin of my woman
She has washed in the river, which is far away
My old woman died
The rattlesnake grows large under the floor of my shack
The buffalo are gone and no one knows where
I smell smoke
The walls of my house are rubber sheets
They quiver when they are touched
The aspen trees outside
Their branches reach upward white
If they could get jobs in the city they would send money to
    their wives
But they wrap themselves in rubber sheets and dream

But there is no cause for alarm just because white rabbits twist
 their necks into question marks
This happens every day in the rubber houses where gangs of heroin
 traffickers squat against the walls practicing self-pollution
And in the morning we shall go down to the sea
Where the long black ships wait
We shall lead the white rabbits by leashes
We shall answer all their questions
Meanwhile Odysseus waits on the beach
On a driftwood log before a fire
The neon cables blue red yellow intense white
Snake forth from the gate of Ilium into the water on both sides
 of him
What was it all for? he wonders
The signs of the musical notes rising up from the beach are black
 and ephemeral
They are mysterious as the stones
He is not Odysseus
He must be called something
He shall be called Enoch
The palm of his hand strokes the irregular edge of the galaxy
And that is just the beginning
When the procession of girls in white gowns approaches in
 the distance
They are an uncountable throng
Their inners thighs rub distractingly together as they walk one inch
 above the stones of the beach
He collapses inward into himself
The further in he goes the bigger he gets
The girl who leads the procession holds a crystal sphere on her
 open hands

He is the sphere
And this is the reason why a rubber band hooked on a nail and stretched to the breaking point
Considers itself fortunate if it finds itself walking with white rabbits into the center of an argument
That is a spider's web glistening with rain and looking through itself into the distance along the beach
At Enoch and Odysseus waiting together on a driftwood log for the procession to arrive
Each girl bearing a lamp
Except the first, who bears the crystal sphere
That in reality is the galaxy the irregular edge of which Enoch strokes with the palm of his hand absent-mindedly
Confident that love will find him

The white deer that walks in the hallway

The white deer that walks in the hallway,
    the deer that was seen by lost children,
its hooves are embroidered with patterns of usury;
    they are memorials of a previous regime.
One remembers this while motorcycling on the causeway
    between hope and the image of white on a wall,
    or the thumbprint of evil and the portrait of an embroideress.
It is so difficult to distinguish the threads from the fabric;
    and your arms brush the dew from the branches of a cedar
    as you walk in a hallway that forever narrows,
or the sunlight from the walls; it is paint flaking,
    as in the prophecies etched on the deer's antlers.

A BREAKER CURLING OVER ONTO THE SHORE

A breaker curling over onto the shore,
I turn to you.
Your breath is in my nostrils,
The smell of you in my hair;
I cannot distinguish my skin from yours.
Hand in hand we walk through walls,
we levitate,
we pass through archways.
The sea is always beneath us,
the sea surges through the archways beneath us,
the sea is in our loins and surges.
We stand by a wall,
the wall is transparent,
beyond it the shore and always the sea.

I do not know why deer wade
up to their knees in blood of doubt

I do not know why deer wade up to their knees in blood of doubt;
    this is the mystery of grace and the tenderness of a rose petal.
A rumor of it passes through the crowds on the street
    like a warm breeze of heresy through the cracks in the window
        panes of the chancellery
    as sticks rattle along the cobblestones.
There is the doorway;
    it leads to the men's room all white porcelain and terraced.
It is difficult to distinguish the urinals from the wash basins;
    one does not want to err on that score;
and the lights are on late in the chancellery,
    it being likely that an attack is planned for the early hours
        of the morning;
    a rumor of it passes through the crowds.
The generals are perched in a row with legs dangling over the
        upper terrace of the men's room;
    they are decidedly opposed to sodomy
    and are vigilant to prevent it,
and they observe closely the patrons
    who are anxious to protect their shoes from the water that
        overflows the trough at the bottom of the wall,
but that is impossible,
and they are uncertain about the blood;
it possibly is menstrual,
though the deer seem unconcerned.

As I Round a Bend in a Canoe a Doe is Swimming

As I round a bend in a canoe a doe is swimming across through the warm brown water.
She sees me and turns back and scrambles up the muddy bank and vanishes into the tamarisk.
Beyond the tamarisk at the bottom of a sandstone cliff are glyphs.
I have read them but forget their meaning.

We should talk, *bon Gérard*

For Gérard de Nerval

We should talk, *bon Gérard*.
We should sit at a café table at the bottom of a sandstone cliff
Beyond the tamarisk that infests the river bank.
We should drink new cider and ponder over the glyphs incised in
    the stone.
We should find arrowheads in the sand and lay them out on the
    table and speak of them.
We should make a sonnet of the glyphs.
We should inscribe the sonnet on an arrowhead
And drop it back onto the sand as we walk on into the
    October night.

Tactical maneuver

fall in and commence the march down the river between the red sandstone cliffs, our feet always two inches above the water. Occasionally one of us steps out of formation to linger at a cliff and scratch a visual record of our march into the patina and must be called back to his duty before his attitude infects the entire platoon, for discipline, though it is not harsh, must be maintained; and loyalty is valued above all, even as we pass through the cottonwoods of a broad, flat bottom off the river, attentive to the encyphered chirpings of the birds and mindful of the traps beneath our feet, for here we must walk on the ground. (You may notice that we are avoiding parataxis insofar as possible.) We were told in the pre-operational briefing that it is suspected that some birds are scouts for the enemy that hides in a side canyon that we were assured we will recognize when we see it. The red birds, the ones that flit among us and pause suddenly without warning an inch before our faces, are the least trusted, but we are not permitted to harm them, for their disloyalty is not yet certain, and it is necessary to retain the good will of the populace. Back on the river (not precisely *on* the river; remember that we march two inches above it), a "Jodie" is heard rising from the rear, one voice at first, then two, and then it is picked up by the whole platoon. Even as we sing, we remain vigilant for traps built into the air through which we march, for the enemy is crafty, and I have seen, in these situations, three men at a time vanish, and either they are never seen again or their corpses are found days later, undeteriorated (autopsies indicating that they have died of asphyxiation only minutes before their corpses are discovered), but naked, their BDUs, which are always freshly laundered, being neatly folded and set on a nearby boulder with their boots atop them neatly laced.

We talk of this when we sit in the shade of cottonwoods eating our meager rations, occasionally throwing a crumb to the red birds (the others never show any interest). Before we reach our destination, I myself step into a trap and find myself sitting alone, waiting, on a high four-legged stool in a complex latrine where all is white porcelain and the urinals and wash basins are built into steeply banked terraces and are difficult to distinguish one from the other and the water in the trough at the bottom of the opposite wall (it might be intended for urination but one cannot be sure) overflows, and I see that it will not be possible to keep water out of my shoes if I risk using it. I do not remember that this was mentioned in the briefing, but I might be mistaken, though I repeatedly review, as I wait, the whole presentation in my mind, endeavoring, insofar as possible, to avoid

I FIND YOU AT THE BOX END

I find you at the box end of a long, winding canyon. The sides are perpendicular and high, and there is no way out, the sides in fact rising so high that they converge in perspective above us. It has been hypothesized that if you could scale any of the three walls you would find that it is a Möbius strip that returns you to your starting point; but a steady stream of dreams issues from the end wall above my head, implying a source beyond the surface of the stone, and flows on back the way I have come. I do not find all of you in one place; you are scattered in parts embedded in the walls; but the parts are soft and warm, definitely flesh, and I am comforted by your presence around me as I feel about with my fingertips on the end wall, seeking the way through.

The old woman who carries a basket on her back

The old woman who carries a basket on her back,
    she has walked far.
She has stories,
    and she will tell them.
Let her sit by the fire,
    let her sit on blankets,
        give her a piece of salmon.
Listen with respect,
    she will tell her stories;
        she will show what she carries in her basket.
She carries stones;
    the stones are words;
they are smoothed by water;
    they have rested on a river bottom a long time.

Do you think God wants to withdraw his ad?

Do you think God wants to withdraw his ad?
Do you think he cares a fig for precedent?
Squeeze an apple till the juice drips from it
See the visions in the drops
They flicker like a TV screen
See the lone figure in the distance
Approaching on an otherwise deserted shore
The water is choppy
It is nervous
The scene is printed on wallpaper
The surface of drift wood is soft
Make a groove in it with a thumbnail
Squeeze an apple till the juice drips from it
God cares nothing for precedent

God is that fat woman in the apron

God is that fat woman in the apron
Standing on the wet concrete floor of a fruit processing plant
Where a child pedals by on a gleaming red tricycle.
The fat woman is old, she has seen much, nothing surprises her.
She watches television at home in her apartment,
Sitting comfortably on a worn sofa,
Hoping for company,
Beer in her refrigerator,
Cookies in her oven.

As we sit together in the living room of the old house

As we sit together in the living room of the old house,
Waiting for someone to be first to speak,
The girl we all recognize arrives with a message.
Printed on white paper is what we do not speak
But all know.

Existenz

Eventually one sleeps and eliminates,
But little else seems quite necessary, although
The longing for sexual release becomes intense, but
Eat? One could simply not take the trouble;
One could take a fetal position and say,
"I prefer not to";
But thirst is another matter,
And few would not recoil from fire.

The sewing machine needle of truth floats free

The sewing machine needle of truth floats free
This is a message written on the underside of leaves
The face peering through the foliage without expression
Painted with streaks black and white
Has been seen examining an assortment of sewing machine needles
The whole cluster of images rises from the depths of a lake
It hovers above streaming downward the letters of the
    Roman alphabet

SNOWFLAKES DISTANCE THEMSELVES FROM THE PRESIDENT

Snowflakes distance themselves from the president
He rides a red tricycle over the horizon
This is to be expected of the vaguely glowing light that rises
    in the well
A series of explosions occurs nightly
But small animals pass on a trail through the grass in an
    endless stream
They are not impressed by clever moves on a checkers board
Nevertheless the game must proceed
Much depends on it
The pieces are enclosed in fur sewed tightly
Tight as the grip of a small hand on the handle of a salt mill
All floating into the night toward the center of the Milky Way

Squanto steps on a dry twig

Squanto steps on a dry twig
The stones in every direction vibrate with the trauma
Even flies disintegrate in the shock wave
The coordinating committee meets on the steps of the Hôtel de
    Ville to discuss strategy
Squanto is late; the senior members are worried
The parking lot is hot and a dried snakeskin is caught in
    a door handle
And they know that every revolution devours its children
And Squanto disperses into the lines of a wiring schematic
His head is a blond revolver

After the next war

After the next war, white arms will grow up from the soil
They will undulate gently and futilely, raised toward the sky
After the next war, we will sit in dark rooms looking out through
    broken glass
We will recall the odor of cinnamon
We will see from the backs of our heads
After the next war, all the TV networks will show endless reruns of
    The Sound of Music
After the next war, ants will emerge endlessly from cracks
    in the walls
The birdbath in the flower garden will dream of becoming
    a sundial
Little girls will write imaginary words in imaginary alphabets on
    picture windows with white lipstick
We will see this through the cracks in the back of our heads
After the next war, the sidewalks will end
                at the water's edge
                in prepositions
                at cliffs' edges
                at the open doors of stripped Buicks
                in premature ejaculations
                at vacant lots where the ground is soft as
                    decayed flesh under the feet
                in midair at the abrupt ends of bridges
                    over water far below
                in the middle of sentences
After the next war I-5 through Seattle will be clogged by

    migrating deer
I-5 will remember working at Boeing
Julie Andrews will stand on a hilltop trying to hold together with
    both hands one breast that is a broken white dinner plate

Staring down a fish

Staring down a fish
Skeins of yellow silk billow up about us
Long ago we made a journey by train
The Logos billowed up from the smoke stack
Across the prairie speeded the black locomotive
The Logos dispersed behind it, one vast herd of silver buffalo
Skeins of yellow silk billowing above them
Through the window of a passenger car staring down a fish

A song for the lady

The Lady's hair flows down from the highest window,
And I am the prince entangled in briars below Her tower,
I am the prince whose eyes are pierced by thorns.
I am the prince who has crossed a desert
To breathe the fragrance of Her hair.
She smiles from above and Her eyes promise,
Her hands are slender as the hopes of winter brides
Whose torsos are wire canary cages.
I loved Her when white clouds of memory
Floated tenderly above deserted streets,
Whispering words that prophesied the fragile days
Of shining beads dangling by single threads.
I am the prince who hides behind Her eyes,
Who hears the song of ancient seas
In the moons that rise from Her fingernails
As she makes a slow pirouette on a fencepost in Kansas.
Her veils hang from the branches of trees,
They remind of promises,
The continuing hope of scattered petals.
Water has risen to Her knees,
But will She reveal the Word?
The Lady wears a gown of dewdrops,
It whispers in the night
Of feathers floating up from a pond,
Of the slow breath of a bell tower
Hidden in a forest of memories,
Of a fluttering of hands

Over a pot of sleeping ferns
She walks in the night among white trunks of aspens,
In moonlight, in snow.
She knows the Word
But does not speak it.
Her cheek is fragrant of apple blossoms,
Her nipples are granite peaks where lightning strikes.
I have walked with her hand in hand
Through corridors hung with pictures.
We emerge onto a plain littered by ruins
Where children in tattered clothes
Sleep in shattered doorways
After the war has passed over them.
Her tears flow,
The ravens that feed on corpses
Nest in Her hair,
Her breasts are distant hills under clouds and rain.
She slips from the hands,
She slips among the aspens,
A bright flash here and there.
She hides in the lake,
She is a fish that eludes the hook,
The fish flash red and gold,
They have swum among the pillars of the temple.
I open my ribcage to invite Her in,
She declines the invitation,
But She looks back
And extends Her hand toward me as She goes—
The Lady who is a poem written in smoke on the face of the moon,
The Lady whose head is a clock face high on a canyon wall,
The Lady whose eyes are the night thoughts of a footfall

    on a stairway,
The Lady whose hands are the wings of a secret turning in the
    shadow of a guitar string
The Lady whose legs are arrows of light shot from a stand of cedars,
The Lady whose mouth is a memory of pear blossoms on a pillow
    of ticking clocks,
The Lady who is the eyes of a cat that sings at the bottom of a well
As birds rise up from a page,
The Lady who has the Epistle to the Hebrews
Tatooed in blue ink at the small of her back,
The Lady who hides behind a mannequin on De Chirico's beach.
But do not tamper with the wheels of Her car—
In Denver there are seven of them,
Gleaming rings
And the sun bright over the Interstate,
The Lady in the passenger seat admiring buttes and canyons.
She is silent as seven crows alight on a power line
On a gyrating morning when the chirping of an over-the-road
    truck
Slips down the spine like a skein of the dew's hair.
I would be a crow reflected in the Lady's eyes,
The tracing of Her finger on that river system
That flows over the edge of the map
After an army has passed over
Leaving children sleeping alone
On beds randomly scattered across a plain
As the Lady descending from her tower walks among them,
Each of her tears a crystal
To be planted in a garden where abandoned memories pray
    for relief
And memories walk beneath trees that grow from the Lady's tears.

For in the beginning is the Lady
Whose feather-fingers lift wind from its hiding place
To the tinkling of tiny bells behind hymns a doorway sings.
Her voice calls black smoke from beyond a distant mountain
To roll thickly across the lake
And sends it back again,
Accompanied by troops of angels masquerading as young girls in party dresses.
She sits apart from the busy crowd,
Mentally tracing the tangle of tributaries
Of that great river that flows beyond the edge of a map.
A hand reaching into the flow slides along the wallpaper leaving four bright streaks,
And the brown snake hiding under the Lady's sheets whispers love songs.
Then what will become of the children of the sun
Who hide under rocks in the alleyways of coastal cities?
They live in walk-up apartments
Where photos of Piaf clipped from magazines cover the walls.
No doubt ivory thighs will play musical chairs
At the next birthday party of a child of the sun,
And words will contort themselves,
The ones that dance on benches
In everlasting hotels solemnly
As the war machine rumbles in the distance,
Lumbers and lurches toward its destiny
In that galaxy-strewn pit that is the past,
As meanwhile I want a kiss,
And it emerges from the lips of the Lady at my shoulder,
White as it hovers in the air between us,
That Lady whose mouth moves silently,

The one who looks backward over Her shoulder
As She proceeds down the hallway
Where She has seen me behind Her in mirrors.
Memory of Her kisses passes through my ribs,
A river through bared roots.
"Wait for the signal," the Lady says,
"From the iron maiden who floats above the loading dock
Where the darkness is shipped out."
The trucks float in tandem over the highway
That slips down the hill into the cloud of music,
That is tiny shards of broken glass.
They fall glittering snow slowly
On the picnic in the grass
Where the iron maiden dolls recall their former happiness
And graffiti on my heart speak of roses and fishhooks
Pouring from broken birds' eggs,
All floating on that river of the well-diggers
Who live on the banks at peace with their tools
And they are not to be disrespected,
Though they hide beneath wings of floral display
Down by the lake where the buttons rise up
On a thin wire toward the spangled sky
From the factory where masks are made
For broken dolls that press their faces gainst the glass
    in automobiles,
Where they are trapped by false premises
And loose pages of forgotten books,
Though no girl was ever ruined by a badly contrived plot,
But random droplets of doubt on rose petals and fishhooks,
That's different.
The Lady knows all this,

This balancing act of lovers on a disintegrating wire,
Leaving a taste in the mouth bitter and yellow,
The symbol of processes that work their way slowly through
    abandoned mine shafts
Where lying on the floor a little man hugs the letter Alpha
    to his body.
The Lady knows all this,
And She knows that it is all out of phase, this collection
    of mutterings
That has sneaked past the guard who examines his legs
For infestations in the hallway of the hotel,
Who knows the way out,
Who has his revenge on the girls who do not,
Though to steal a kiss from one of them
Is difficult as the equations written among the stars.
The Lady knows all this,
And also cords braided by hypothetical grasshoppers
Weaving themselves among the roots of grass.
But I cannot think
That when wind is caught kissing a broken window pane
That is more disturbing than the dissolution of tires
Caught *en flagrante delicto* behind a service station
With the burnt-out clutch of a pickup,
And barbarians swarm across the frozen river,
I sitting on the hither bank watching,
Wrapped in red rags,
Comforted by the memory of my open hand
On the warmth of an upper thigh
When the river, broad and slow,
Flows through the city toward the open sea,
The barbarians parading on the boulevard along the quay,

Their banner of bloody ice raised before them on a pole,
And we sit on a grassy hilltop
Under a sun that oozes yellow drops.
The crows dodge them,
But we hide inside a clock,
The cogs of the wheels the edges of Her teeth on my tongue,
And the bowl from which black words rise up in single file
Is an old shoe.
Its laces have strangled innocent men
On scaffolding erected on the fears of lonely dogs,
On the hopes of children who sit patiently on pews
In the nave of a ruined basilica,
On seats in a train that speeds through European nights
After a war has smashed all the dear little glass houses,
Their fragments scattered on a beach,
Soon to be covered by rising tide.
They are the color of rubies,
But we are safe,
Locked as we are inside a clock,
The gears of which are polished every night
After we have declared our love anew to the stairwells.
Hand in hand we walk through ruby mists
Exhaled by real flowers in imaginary gardens.
There was a garden in the basilica
Where birds crawled through on all fours,
Exhausted by interminable games
Of croquet with the Queen of Hearts;
Though she is a sweetheart,
Much defamed in old books
That are wastes of melting snow within.
And that garden was not imaginary—

It was real as the dreams of the small brown snakes
That sleep in the drainpipes of decayed infatuations.
But hand in hand we walk now,
I wondering silently when she might finally place my hands
On the ridges of a bas-relief sculpted on a wall,
The answer to the riddle of portraits etched on snow,
Or when the ruby will burst,
The fragments glittering about the head of a marble bust
Crying out in pleasure
When the river that flows from the bottom of the doorpost
Mingles with roots of bracken fern
In the ancient soil of radiant streets
Littered with misaddressed dispatches
From the war with the sphynxes,
And in the square surrounded by temples and palaces,
A jetting fountain of small black seeds at the center,
One encounters four old women emerging headfirst
From the top of a writing table,
And the war strolling untroubled through the park,
Startling into flight a covey of cherry blossoms.
The Lady has seen this,
And She has seen the violets that say "All in a day's work,"
The violets that pick their way down the sides of bell towers,
"Though we can never know the end results of our labors."
The shawl that covers the head of the bell keeper's wife
Is a tissue of empty cigarette packages.
They jug jug their way through the scene,
They never rehearse,
But the violets are conscientious,
Dreaming of streets in remote Brazilian villages
Where fishermen drag their boats through the central plaza.

They stack them in the ballrooms of glass houses
Where violets watch from attic windows,
And the logic of a sea swell reflects a glint of desire from
 a grass blade
Rooted in the memory of floating above a rising tide sluicing
Swelling through Midtown Manhattan.
It carries all statues, marble,
Sprouting grass luxuriantly.
And the Lady reminds me of
The image printed on the face of a sandstone cliff in Yosemite Park,
On shirts and underthings hanging from a clothesline on a
 tenement balcony,
Though there are no sandstone cliffs in Yosemite Park,
This according to birdsongs heard in the night,
Thoughts of sealed semis barreling down highways of
 forgotten destructions.
They are all made of glass,
Like the dire wolf of our childhood,
Its detached paws secreted in the pocket of a white candle
That is switched on only for birthdays,
Bought at Walmart and in questionable taste.
Mother has dealings with the dire wolf every Christmas
When the box of ornaments is pulled from beneath the stairs
And a glass house materializes suddenly in the woods.
The wolf is suspicious,
He is filled with foreboding,
For all his war plans are depicted on the walls
For all passersby to see,
And the white light that glows within keeps its secrets.
Pockets, pockets,
And the mystery of old machinery in a patch of dry grass,

Of lines of glistening black seeds radiating from the navel
Of an artificial candle in questionable taste.
Pockets, pockets,
Unheard by the transparent cube that revolves above these hills,
My love for the Lady impaled to a tree,
Crying out urgently as scarlet feathers quivering with dread
Of another game of croquet with the Queen of Hearts.
But at the last moment we all escape down the hole that opens in the nearest hill,
Grasping at a door handle of a gleaming red Buick
And fingering idly the hair that sprouts from the seat covers.
The driver described as of average height.
He is fully documented,
And he considers the choices escaped from the bird cages,
But no crime has been committed,
No charges can be brought,
For the birds have long since flown,
And the star map that slips from beneath the dashboard is already factored into the plan,
And later, when the girls from the mask factory exit through the many doors,
They walk hand in hand two by two to their apartments in the cages,
Dark silhouettes in the fog.
Each holds a mask before her face—
So important to hide the white down that billows from every orifice of their heads—
And desire coils about the Lady's legs.
They are cascades of coins.
She lingers beside the highway,
Arms thrust deep into the wall behind Her,

Wall of paper cups and musical notations,
A sonata of white feathers,
Her midriff white feathers,
No solid place to lay hands.
She kissed me once behind the wall,
Shadows there sharp-edged, sun harsh.
Trying to hold Her by the waist,
Hands grope among the feathers,
And She spoke of Dante,
Who crouches beneath the Golden Arches,
Draws his cowl over his head—
Four lanes of traffic have undone so many.
He has an appointment at two with the white annelid that lives in a white Styrofoam cup
In the gutter with a crumpled paper napkin white as the bridal gown of Bice,
As a fungus on the trunk of a rain-soaked fir.
The light changes and the traffic moves,
And the night dabs a tear from beneath its left eye.
The big guns are pulled up to the line,
And the *Atlas of the Great War* has photographs of all this,
Compiled many years after the last regiment marched into the sea,
Down the main street between the rows of empty shops
And the girls with empty eyes and shawls drawn over their heads,
A yellow tulip held by the stem in the teeth of each.
New regiments appear on the far ridges,
But before they reach the village the soldiers grow wings and fly off with the pigeons.
The girls' eye sockets are hollow—
Run a fingertip around inside them.
And the Lady has told me of fishhooks crawling in tandem,

Losing all self-control before the beauty of archways to heaven
Between the eyelids of a window.
But the girls who flutter their eyebrows like peahens
    in a snowstorm
Recollect nothing of LPs, 33 1/3 RPM,
Jazz mostly, and R&B.
But then the trash barrels stored in the moon's pudenda
Think of themselves as Currier & Ives prints,
The ones that lay themselves down on deserted pavement
Under skies black but brightly spangled,
And the professor of military history,
Who specializes in trench warfare,
Pats himself on the behind.
He is a glutton but loved by the tiny women
Who line up for a firing squad
Against the floor-molding of the classroom.
She has told me of this,
And of snow that falls inside the clock,
The clock behind the door,
The clock that hides beneath the wings
Of a wounded angel left behind after the war,
The war between the sphinxes that was won by a free flow of cheap
    but glittering information
Through the alleyways of the sun and along the beaches
    next to the water.
It is now locked up in iron boxes
Held tenderly on the laps of young girls,
The ones with green hair that sprouts from their faces.
Comb it gently and it whispers of lost loves
That entwine themselves mindlessly in coils of the sleeping offal
And the cast-off clothing of recalcitrant nuns,

The ones who refuse to make the secret signs
To suffering flowers behind the eclipse,
The ecliptic draining away unnoticed.
The loss of it will come as a shock
When the troops returning home from the war
Fall down one by one in the middle of the square,
Or of the city council meeting—
It could go either way.
The Lady knows.

Composition in two movements

I

We sit regarding silently the dying fire,
I and my companions,
Thinking on things that come to mind unbidden
And often unwelcome in such a circumstance,
In the small opening among fir trees
Tall and old of a forest so vast
That none of us has more than a vague sense,
An assumption that we sometimes consider re-examining,
Briefly and with an unease similar to what comes to us—
To me at least,
And I suppose that I am not so different from my companions,
For we have grown up together,
A time when we were not together being beyond recall,
And we being sometimes not certain
Where one ends and the other begins—
Similar, I was saying, to what comes to us when we recall
    or imagine
Sitting on a wooden chair in a shaft of sunlight
That comes through a window of a house of indeterminate size,
Darting our eyes furtively to one side
Toward a doorway opened inward,
The door having an intricately worked knob,
An open doorway through which are visible
The landing and the upper portion of the balustrade
Of a stairway with a smoothly carved ornamental sphere
Affixed on the corner,

Voices heard from below,
Not angry,
Merely discussing calmly our future,
Though we only surmise it,
Never quite making out the words,
And we imagine that,
If we could float—
And here I wish we had in English a true subjunctive case—
Above the scene around the fire,
We would rise higher and higher into the night air,
Looking down on the fire
As it receded to become a mere point of light
Not unlike the stars,
And in every direction see dimly through the darkness,
Lighted only by the stars
(Which are, it must be acknowledged, preternaturally bright),
The forest falling below the horizon,
And hear the soft soughing
Of the wind in the fir boughs,
So difficult to distinguish
From the sound of running water;
The things that come to mind also
When one walks alone through a suburban subdivision
On smooth and clean concrete sidewalks
Under clear sky on warm days
When the breeze carries grit blown up
From nearby construction sites,
From which come the sounds of heavy machinery,
And a crumpled sheet of white paper
Skitters along the street parallel to the gutters,
In one of which runs a trickle of water,

One of the homeowners evidently
Having carelessly left his lawn sprinkler running too long;
One of those things being—
And you knew this was coming;
You need not pretend otherwise—
what a neighbor girl let us see but not touch
When we were twelve,
In a subdivision not unlike this one,
For some things never change,
And I finally admit to myself
That the time to go has passed
And stand and shoulder my possible bag,
Which we still call by that term,
Aware of the anachronism,
Being nostalgic about such things,
For there were good times then,
The memory of which is evoked by the smell of smoke
Or the flash of a white tail in the underbrush
Beneath the fir trees,
And I turn my back to the fire
And continue down the narrow but discernable trail,
More discernable now that the light is rising
(For dawn will come),
Deeper into the forest,
Though I am not certain that we are going deeper in,
For we may already have passed the deepest place
And are now moving outward toward the edge
Opposite from where we entered,
If we have not, in fact, merely become disoriented,
Though I suspect that this is one of those forests that,
The further in you go,

The bigger it gets—
And I have also known houses like that,
And women—
A small twinge of embarrassment
And regret concerning the neighbor girl
Hovering at the edge of consciousness
Like a tiny, bright, and troublesome fly,
Though greater shames and regrets awaited;
Grateful as I am at these times
For the unfailing loyalty of my companions,
Who silently rise and fall in behind me in single file,
These companions who never speak in my condemnation,
Though at times they stand nearby looking on,
The corners of their lips rising in the faintest
Of knowing and sympathetic and sad smiles,
As do mine, gentle reader, *mon frére,*
At your denials;
And I confess that the days are sometimes long,
Though none longer than that one on which,
Early in the morning,
Descending a long, barely perceptible decline,
We broke out of the trees
Into a wide meadow of fresh grass and white daisies
Where near the center a group of young people
Who sat in a half circle on collapsible chairs,
Being led, as it was explained to us, in a discussion of—
And here memory fails me,
Though when I reminisce on this incident
An image presents itself of a wall
In the stairwell of that house
Where we sat in the shaft of sunlight,

And of words scrawled on the walls
As we descended the staircase,
With artist's charcoal,
A whole phrase, in fact,
That one of my companions reminds me
Once served as the three-dimensional intersect
Of a text by Aloysius Bertrand
And another by an anonymous Jew of third century Alexandria
Concerning certain points of Old Kingdom astronomy;
Though, notwithstanding, the instructor called for chairs
For me and my companions,
And we sat through the morning and afternoon
And into the evening,
Finding it necessary, after the class was concluded
And the participants by twos,
Girls and boys,
Drifted off toward the staircase at the edge of the meadow,
We watching them with twinges of envy,
To bed down where we were,
In the military surplus sleeping bags that we carried,
Without a fire,
Because it would have been a shame to mar
What was so nearly virgin meadow,
I never ceasing to hope,
Secretly of course,
Because the thought is so childish,
That such small self-denials might be accepted as penance
(And here again I wish for a true subjunctive case).
Later, descending the stairway behind the students,
We recognize some of the markings on the wall
Recognize the pattern, that is,

Having observed it in the configuration of black flint stones
Marking pathways across Death Valley,
During those years that spiral around the neck
Of the giraffe that camouflages itself in a patch of wild violets,
Or in the memory of waiting for hours at the DMV
For our number to come up—
Those stones, I was saying,
That ultimately trickled off into the distance,
Hopelessly
(But maybe only apparently so;
else what is grace for?)—
Hopelessly, I was tempted to say,
Out of reach,
Like the pleasure that verges on pain
Of descent into that chasm of *magie sugestive*.
That was where the pathway marked by the black flint stones
Led in the end,
After all our hypothesizing and argumentation.
It was like this—
As we were returning together to the States
To muster out after the end of the most recent war
(I will never say the *last* war),
We signed on with another recruiter
To join a journey of discovery
On an expedition into Death Valley's canyons of grace.
One objective of the expedition
Was to identify and document
Species of cactus unique to those canyons.
That particular project had been under discussion for years,
Many years,
Beyond the recall of the oldest living members of the society,

One of the older members nonetheless
Insisting that he had seen a drawing,
A faded, smudged pencil sketch,
Of a certain variety of *Opuntia*,
Which a note scribbled at the bottom of the paper said
Was copied from a book
That the artist had read when he was a boy,
Sitting for many hours in a worn upholstered chair
Set in a corner of the landing
Of a staircase in his childhood home,
Next to a bookcase filled with old volumes
With titles that he never, ever saw in the local public library.
I never had an opportunity to ask that older member
If he had seen written somewhere on that paper,
Maybe on the back,
A description of any markings,
Or any lines,
Drawn on the walls of that staircase,
But, despite the lack of that confirmation,
I felt a strong sense of duty
That impelled me to sign on with the expedition,
And, moreover, the description of the chair
On the landing next to the bookcase
Resonated deeply with me,
Evoking as it did a memory of the neighbor girl
In a thin blue cotton dress
Sitting on a similar chair
And holding in her lap with both hands,
Taking care not to prick her fingers on the spines,
A specimen of that very variety of *Opuntia*.
The neighbor girl.

Yes.
We keep returning to that.
And it is necessary to confess
That with the embarrassment and regret
There is also a memory of joy in discovery
(and a truly subjunctive case would be very useful here).

2

The sword fern that grows from my ribcage
Knows it is late for an appointment,
But the women who turn themselves inside out
To reveal the labyrinthine hallways within
Are indifferent to the fact,
And indeed they drag themselves across the floor,
Having lost their bodies below the ribcage,
Fragmentary reveries of rabbits
Who live in the grass beneath stairways.
When they speak they say,
"Go on to perfection,
Not laying again the foundation,
But be still and hear the music
Flow forth from the cliff face
Through that opening partway up,
Where the map and the terrain
That are one thing become separate things,
Where a rabbit with a Sten concealed in its fur
Speaks of cherry trees and yellowed envelopes,
And equations blush with self-consciousness."
But then the scissor that revolves inside an eyeball

Is a stray dream that wanders in that forest of symbols,
Smelling treason and the fear of lost children.
"This is not what I expected,"
A female voice is heard to say
From out of sight in the next room.
And then a watercolorist dangles his participles
Over a sheet of white paper.
Poor bait they are,
But the fish in any case are indifferent at this hour.
They swim desultorily just beneath the surface of the paper.
The watercolorist rises at noon every day,
Replaces his participles in his tackle box,
and says, "Let us return to the topic of the virgins in violet,"
Evoking the day we walked into that wet forest,
When the tears of tulips cringed
Behind a fountain of curling fern tips,
When sand flowed between the fingers
Of ten virgins in violet
Who remembered the way to the Quay d'Orsay,
And the smell of wet cedar permeated all equations.
And then the little man sat
On the edge of the urinal that is too high to use,
Up there you say,
Where the wall is encrusted with petrified roses.
"Their flesh was tender once," you say,
"In that night when the alphabet swirled in the flushing water."
The little man recites the first Psalm backward,
And you say you will meet me where the first line
Wraps around a corner in Helvetica.
You say, "Encrusted, tender,"
And "Read a sealed book," you say,

As you slide open the drawer of your right breast.
The pages have the consistency of the handful of spiders
That normally reside in the drawer.
Each letter hangs in space,
Its edges distinct to the touch,
Each holding its fate in its hands
With the self-assurance of a fragment of apple peel
On which for so long a white horse has galloped joyfully,
And then splitting the tree open with both hands—
Thick bark, yellow-white wood.
It splits clear through,
Blue sky beyond.
I knew a girl like that
Who covered her head with a shawl
As she led her lambs homeward.
Sometimes the tree grows from a bed of music.
Fingers on her bare back play melodies
That dance in the space opened in the tree,
Blue sky behind them.
Kiss the girl and she is an uncompleted sentence,
And the dreams of a snake
(Whether venomous I cannot say)
Flicker in the ether in Technicolor.
Two trees flicker in and out of sight.
The snake iridesces.
Moments like these are precious
As a necklace of rabbits' teeth
And indifferent to that fact
In the afterglow of battle
With the eyes that watch suspiciously
From the writing table in the corner.

"Not what I expected,"
The female voice is again heard to say.
To what is their suspicion to be attributed?
For though my guilt is certain
I do not attempt to conceal it.
And incidentally, a specimen of *Opuntia,* it was,
At the joining place of her spread legs,
And she would not let me touch it;
But sometimes we sat naked
Side by side on the edge of a cliff,
Our bare heels touching the sandstone face
(Warm, it was, and gritty against our skin)
As we watched a vast lake
Drain out between convulsing hills.

The posting

Children menaced by a broken light bulb
Dream of a cobblestoned street
The old woman watching from the balcony remembers the wars
She is said to be a witch but her arms are made of chicken bones
The street is somewhere in Rumania
We are responsible for this fact at examination time

I jot those lines while traveling by train to a new posting somewhere eastward. My orders cannot specify the final destination because the line of battle is constantly moving. Also, it is somewhat uncertain in which army I am enlisted. I hope I will recognize it when I see it, no doubt by some detail of the uniform. Or maybe I will ask the girl I am keeping in my duffle bag. She wears a red, rather tight, high-waisted skirt that does not compliment her figure, as it calls attention to her waist, which is a little thick. She is otherwise quite attractive, and she promises to assist me on my journey in any way she reasonably can if I will smuggle her onto the train. We met at the dead end of a cobblestoned street where we had been walking on opposite sides, not speaking to each other until we had simultaneously come to the wall at the end, which we had not recognized as a wall from a distance because on it was painted a highly realistic scene of storefronts extending in perfect perspective to a white sand beach and beyond that a blue white-capped sea on which boats sailed in the distance. I had entertained some notion of deserting and escaping by boat, or of finding employment at one the carnival booths that I had been told were set up along the beach out of site around the corners of the last buildings, and the reality was disappointing. She was wearing black high heels that struck the sidewalk resoundingly. We both were surprised when we struck the wall, and that led to conversation. I had no alternative but to board the train, and she had no better option than to be smuggled on in my duffle bag. She discerned my fleeting thought of making love to her, smiling and telling me good naturedly, "Do not sacrifice what you want most for what you want now." After the conductor had passed through she got out of the bag and sat beside me on the hard wooden seat. That was when I noticed that one of her arms was made of chicken bones, and I was surprised that I hadn't noticed before, because she was wearing a short-sleeved blouse (white, have I mentioned that?). After we arrive at my destination, she tells me that she has changed her mind about making love, but she is stopped from accompanying me by a guard at the turnstile at the entrance to the tunnel that leads to the trench where I will find my army. On the walls are depicted some of the images that I jotted down while on the train, and also a map in white paint of the tunnel maze ahead of me, which I will need to explore to find the battle.

Poem kit; some assembly required

last night when the odor of hatred rose up
your hand that earlier held the umbrella
the one the virgins ate
but your hand—small, delicate
of birds, tin cans, outdated maps
your hand lying open on a table
the white marble one
where the odor of hatred rises up
I remembered you
smoke of a candle
over the jeweled swan
after separating flowers from feathers
furtive in pursuit through the many arches
bicyclists along the rim of a canyon
detached from your statue in the corner
on the riverbank
twisting thread of white smoke
and bright knives

Snowflakes float out from the center point

Snowflakes float out from the center point of existence
(like that Shakespeherian Rag
O O O O)
A white knee protrudes from the sand and sings silent melodies
like a paper doll abusing itself under the stairs
Love goes up the chimney blue like cigarette smoke
and I am lost somewhere between a freeway
and an alley that climbs the wall like a mad capitalist
Is this what words have come to?
Yalu nang flicha, mete na singa ka, mete na falun ka
A straight razor sliding smoothly over the surface of a yellow
    balloon
is love swelling within my ribcage
stroking the lamb chop of satisfied desire
tenderly.
Yalu nang flicha, mete na singa ka, mete na falun ka
A crow flying over the Black Hills looks down upon the
    encampment
the lodges glowing red as coals as they prepare to levitate
And I am lost somewhere between a freeway and a dumpster
    behind a 7-Eleven
Yalu nang flicha, mete na singa ka, mete te falun ka
When Black Elk was a boy there was no bus station under Third
    Mesa
Yalu nang
What words have come to

The doorknob of the Logos

The doorknob of the Logos
(As you teeter on the edge of an Apocalypse of Enoch)
Is a breast with a nipple that tastes of wild rose blossom
Wear it on your lapel as you climb the rocks toward Chief Joseph's
    last encampment
It is a safe-conduct pass
It will come in handy when the cavalry arrives with doom
    in its hatband
Back to the Apocalypse of Enoch:
It winds like a snake through a labyrinth of drumbeats

A MIST OF EQUATIONS

A mist of equations exhaled by the Unnamed wraps itself around a lamppost,
Down in the valley of indecision
Where I go at night to see ferns curled in ecstasy
And small memories pour from my fingertips,
A cloud of spilled alphabet,
And visions of gleaming bone tease the roots of mushrooms
Hiding in the deeper recesses of whiteness—the doorknob says,
The one set into the bark of an alder tree,
The bark that whispers "Open me!" as I glide in darkness through the woods
And the tongue twists in the wind that blows from the sea over a darkened village,
A miasma of memory that fragments into stones on the shore,
Each stone holding the memory of young girls
Whose frothing breath plants daffodils in the craters of the moon
And nails an eye to a fencepost in Kansas,
An ax in a woodshed splitting infinitives lengthwise.
Far down the road an albino giraffe waits outside a house
Where the supreme generals of opposing armies negotiate a cease-fire,
Their lower legs encased in cardboard imitation snakeskins.
All the parties involved are aware that white birds nest in chimneys of incandescent row houses
Where discarded skins of prehistoric snakes wipe the noses of abandoned children

And the better angels of our nature cavort with sphynxes left over
    from the late Jurassic,
And equations coalesce.
They are a wet film on a white wall inside a house on an
    upper floor,
In the center of the wall a black object the size and shape of a clay
    pigeon waiting to be pressed,
And when it is pressed the wall will vanish,
And there will be revealed the final secret,
The place from where all things flow out from the Unnamed.
It is rumored to be a virgin sitting crosslegged beneath a streetlight
Dragging her fingers through the red and black greasepaint
    on her cheeks,
Remembering a feathered evening when the melody that trickled
    unnoticed along the gutter
Emitted an odor of clover
    in sunlight.
This is before the flayed carcass hiding among the sunflowers
Cries out silently for recognition by the passing columns,
The army of winter and shining buttons that hides in piles of
    yellowed dry goods receipts
When the farm cat goes prowling.
And always the birds flow,
Slithering about the drainpipe on an ivy-covered wall,
Birds dreaming of arrows caught in the slipstream of history,
Begging for mercy from a crowfooted crone
Who licks up the spittle of dogs in the center of the street.
This is a cause for grief that perches on a powerline between two
    crows in rain,
The eternal concavity of memory that evokes a steaming
    locomotive on the distant horizon.

Meanwhile, a word rises from a well.
Its wings bear the child of the Woman crowned with the Sun to
    sandstone canyons, buttes, mesas.
A face rises from a canyon floor engraved on a chocolate coin from
    a Christmas stocking.
I lay myself down by the side of a river, clear and slow and warm.
Memory of better days hovers over my face, a swarm of mosquitos.
All this is written on a red cliff near the ground, behind a boulder.
The words flow down, a thin stream along the ground,
    into the river.
They rejoice to be free,
And the resident teaching anthropologist is a female impersonator
Who cannot be deceived in matters of criminal investigation,
But there are those who try,
Whose lies are graceful pirouettes on the loading dock.
It is lonely out there and quiet.
A single lamp on a tall pole lights it,
And the furthest edge is in the darkness,
Where a head is transfixed by a pigeon feather above the river of
    manhole covers
That flows from the armpit of a lonely streetwalker.
She flutters in the wind,
A tatter pinned to a clothesline,
Embroidered with the alphabet of the darkling beetles.
They march in ordered ranks across the unseen street,
Trusting in the map that is scratched on the hood of the
    lead vehicle.
The tattered streetwalker also drags her finger tips down her
    painted cheeks.
She is Gaugin's favorite concubine sitting naked on the ground
    beside a broken birdbath,

Knees up and arms wrapped about them,
Dry grass protruding from beneath her toenails.
The lock dial on her chest—
Who remembers the combination?
The door would open to sunlight,
Warm on grassy hills,
Ravens turning against the blue.
We would walk there hand in hand,
But I have forgotten the combination.
And where is the hand that turns the dial?
Memory is a broken crystal vase,
The combination scattered with the fragments.
Among other memories of things that never happened
Is a coupling with a gaunt and lonely woman in a weathered shack
   on the prairie.
A windmill turns behind the shack.
She has red hair and is silent in her ecstasy.
The sun burns in a cloudless sky,
But a breeze through open windows dries the skin,
And torn pages of a mail-order catalog are scattered on the floor.
The memory is printed on a catalog page,
And on the reverse side is a picture of two children playing on a
   swing set
In the back yard of a small suburban house.
They also do not exist.
This is of no moment,
As the grass that grows from the beneath the concubine's fingernails
Is dry as the rust on the machine that rests on the parlor floor.
It collapses to the touch into a tangle of Erector Set parts,
And a pearl astonished by the eruption of its own pubic hairs
Dangles from the septum of the concubine,

Whose portrait etched on snow lifts its head to inhale a
    remembered happiness
On a crumpled sheet white as the conscience of a galaxy
Imploding under stress from fear of loss.
The pearl speaks:
"This pattern of streets radiating from the center of the sheet
Is beautiful as a collapse of table legs in an attic."
The pearl is a pale leg crooked around a doorpost
In a time when a striped multicolored fish circular as a
    pregnant thought
Watches without expression gasping lovers
In bas relief on the surface of a sea (hypothetical).
They consist of several pieces strategically arranged on a
    soft chessboard
Circular as a pregnant thought (hypothetical)
And the next war comes calling beribboned in yellow,
Sauntering through the gate unconcerned with ceremony.
Troupes of tiny women scatter before it.
They stand on kitchen counters counting the bodies that issue
    from the war's bowels,
And in the otherwise deserted street children with stumps of arms
    and legs
Listen for remembered songs.
Tatters of songs.
Dry grass beneath fingernails.

Elk that wraps its antlers in skeins of yellow silk

Elk that wraps its antlers in skeins of yellow silk—
It dreams in the night,
Far below the sidewalk that flows from the storefronts,
A river of darkness and light
That is a target for sharpshooters in the early hours.
I touch your lips in memorial.
I pray for release from the prison of iron nails,
Of the Teletype scroll of nostalgia,
Covered from edge to edge
With a shorthand that was taught in Oklahoma,
In the hills,
Where red dirt equivocates shamelessly and endlessly.
This is doubt.
This is right.
This is loneliness.
This is a small black seed on a white porcelain saucer
Set beside a vase of sunflowers
And voices that murmur just out of sight.

In Quito, Ecuador

In Quito, Ecuador, girls stand about in disconnected groups on the shores of lakes, opening their minds to the slightest of breezes. This phenomenon is characteristic of sunflowers also, the ones that stand about in disconnected groups on the stairways of interstellar movie theaters. The lakes are scattered randomly among tenement houses, on the outer walls of which flicker black-and-white movies thought by most film historians to have been long lost. A favorite of the girls is a travelogue featuring Venice West, California, in the day when body builders lifted barbells on the sand alongside the old boulevard and competing loudspeakers played Lawrence Welk and Charlie Parker. Quito, Ecuador, sinuates through the streets, becoming hopelessly entangled among the tenement houses but remaining untroubled as it hums to itself Lawrence Welk's tunes and taps its fingers to Charlie Parker's rhythms and the stairways among the stars wait nostalgically for the girls again to ascend and descend, softly.

The Being that contains all things

The Being that contains all things—
That is, the herd of deer that—
That is, the woman on the loading dock who opens her arms
To cast a cloud of spangles into the sunlight—
She is a door ajar,
She is the breeze of memory that ripples the surface of a lake,
Fish golden and red flashing,
Hiding behind the door,
A chair also remembering,
A deer embraced about the neck.

The smell of a clean cotton dress

The smell of a clean cotton dress freshly ironed
This is where the girls come in dancing on a clothesline
They spin effortlessly
As the words of the *Encyclopedia of Philosophy* drain out
　upon them

Lactation of a white marble statue

Lactation of a white marble statue runs in fine rivulets among alders in canyons of grace where dogs chasing deer are dressed in fine linens, where the River Grijalva bears bodies to the sea and a prophet sleeps on a pillow of gold plates. This is counterintuitive to soldiers lost in a mist of snowdrops, but do not think it strange—it is engraved on a 33 1/3 rpm disk from the era of cool jazz, rare but not strange.

And we walk among the alders

And we walk among the alders
And the deer are cautious
But willing to give us the benefit of doubt
As we walk on points of needles four feet high
Stepping carefully from one to the next
They rise through the mulch and the underbrush one by one
To meet our feet as we step forward

The sad song of derangement

The sad song of derangement
Extends through filaments of pain
On which birds of cloud and frothy milk
Perch through violet nights
And chess pieces of memory flirt in the hallways
With maidens who walk and mock,
A four-position dial-type lock hanging from the neck of each
By a black velvet ribbon imprinted with an abstract of her case.
A maiden emerges from the door of a cottage,
Sets up two chairs,
Says, "Sit, let us talk."
A four-position dial-type lock hangs from her neck.
It also is made of cloud and frothy milk.

The Watchers on the hills
wring their hands in anguish

The Watchers on the hills wring their hands in anguish.
It begins in the spring,
When white elk bones protrude from the soil.
It begins when dreams lurking behind wallpaper
Sing out their pleas for a quarter here, a dollar there,
Anything to get them through the famine to follow the next war.
The Watchers wring their hands
As they recall the time when they walked among the pines and the cedars in troupes,
Leisurely as the fragrance rising from broken rowboats stacked on the banks of rivers
Descending from—they forget the exact place, but it was far and high.
The fragrance rises leisurely as the giraffe wearing the neckless of emeralds of dubious authenticity
Finds its footing on that thin wire that stretches between credulity and faith
Over the deepening abyss of certainty where black ships sail,
Where fishermen throw out their jewels,
Where doves that dwell under arches,
Crumbling arches through which armies passed during the last war
Leaving behind smoke and desolation and starving children
And women who wander alone about the yellow plain
Where black shapes sit out the long empty day.
A splendid door of black, polished wood and brass fittings
On which is tacked a child's crayon drawing of his parents

Hangs above the far hills against turbulent clouds white as a
    fish belly.
It is a rumor of the coming circus,
Of the gypsy trapeze artist and the bearded woman,
Of the opening of gates to deeper secrets,
Though there are deeper still,
Deep within redrock cliffs above the plain where the
    women wander.
Up from a well they rise on slips of notepad paper:
Agonizing decisions made by bears in the throes of hibernation,
Beavers that raise pendants red, yellow, white, and black over their
    dams beneath the freeways,
Images of buttons pink and plastic,
Forgotten words of forgotten prophets,
The secrets faithfully kept by the old women who stir the kettles,
The secrets of the prophets who dwell with the bears,
The red, yellow, white, and black pendants sewn into quilts to
    wrap about the old women.
The old man sitting on the ground leaning against a broken wall,
He remembers when he stood before a wall of sandstone etching
    characters into the patina,
Letters of a language once known,
A language of troupes of players in a play once known,
Before the darkness rose from the sea and spread across the beach
    and then the village and then the farms and the forests and
    mountains behind it.

The deer serene

The deer sleep serene in the knowledge that the white sheet that covers them has been thoroughly vetted by the generals that patrol the lavatories where conferences are held daily to decide the fate of nations and pearl divers, but the Book of Revelation regards its predecessors as fully competent to decide the fate of pencil sharpeners and plastic rulers in the third-grade classrooms of all the world.

Note to a young Mormon poet

Wherefore seeing we also are compassed about
With so great a cloud of witnesses,
Let us not fear to surrender to the river
That bears us through the window in a red cliff
To the house where a red wind breathes
Across a beach toward a sea of remembrance
And small birds perched on wires of light
Push their boats before them as in sad songs.

A boy sits at a table

A boy sits at a table in an immense library filled with shelves of large and heavy books. In these books are all the secrets that forever draw us on and forever elude us. Before him on a table a book lies open and inviting him to read, and he reads, but afterward he remembers only fragments of sentences, even of words: "the key that unlocks the door of," "ington has painted," "ewise," "a girl's shoe lying in the hallway."

Exchanging white stones engraved with our names

Exchanging white stones engraved with our names,
We join the procession into the sun.

Author's note

Most of my likely readers will find the poems in the first part of this collection, approximately through "Outside the Longhouse," to be readily accessible, but those in the latter part of the book may seem puzzling and strange—"surrealistic," though I am not a Surrealist (Neo-Romanticist influenced by Surrealism is closer to the mark). If the reader finds a beauty in those poems, despite their seeming irrationality, and though it be a mysterious beauty, then I call them successful. My method for composing them has been an exercise of something like what Keats called "negative capability," which I understand as a stepping back of the conscious, controlling mind with its categories and preconceptions to allow the poem to emerge from "somewhere else." It is similar to Mallarmé's method, and also the Surrealists', as described by Wallace Fowlie: "To give over all initiative to the words themselves" (*Mallarmé,* Phoenix Books, 1962). I suggest that they be approached as dreams. Every reader will have had the experience of waking with a dream that seems important and meaningful, though the full meaning might remain elusive. Some of the imagery in these poems, in fact, came from sleeping dreams. Most of them, however, are more like waking dreams. I view dreams as messages from a deeper part of our being, the "unconscious," if you will, supplying insights to assist us in the conscious conduct of life. I entertain the possibility that such messages are revelatory in a certain sense, for they come from a place within us that, by God's grace, is uncorrupted by the Fall. The unconscious always speaks the truth of its insights and evaluations about matters on which at the conscious level "the natural man," as it is called in the Book of Mormon (Mosiah 3:19), is too willing to equivocate, rationalize, and deny. The "I" in the mortal conscious mind wants to cheat, but the unconscious is unfailingly honest. Whether messages from my unconscious are of value to anyone but me, the reader will decide, but my sense is that my life's tasks are not wholly unlike those of others, and I become more persuaded to the Jungian view that a common set of archetypal figures from a collective unconscious speaks in dreams to us all, and, because we share the "human condition," what is spoken to one might be of value to another. As Joseph Campbell has put it, the myth is the public dream, the dream is the personal myth. I would add that the public myth must begin in someone's personal myth.

More can be said about the nature of these oneiric poems (which is what I prefer they be called), but to say it with anything approaching completeness requires far more philosophical and theological verbiage than space available here permits, and to condense it renders it even more cryptic than it is in fuller discourse. Nevertheless, I think I must say something, and it is the following: to my mind, poems of this kind can be merest glimpses through a window on the infinite and eternal and marvelous and, rationally, literally unspeakable mystery of being, of "that which is Spirit, even the Spirit of truth," in the words of Joseph Smith (Doctrine and Covenants 93:23); of the utter freedom—agency—of Being; of the erotic and convulsively beautiful ecstasy of Eternal Life and Creation.

BIOGRAPHICAL NOTE

Colin Blaine Douglas was born in 1944 and brought up in Western Washington; is an enrolled member of the Samish Indian Nation; became a Latter-day Saint at the age of sixteen; served in the Brazilian Mission 1964–1966; served in Military Intelligence in the Regular Army and the Utah National Guard, retiring as sergeant first class; attended the University of Washington as a journalism major and received a bachelor's degree in psychology and a master's degree in American literature at Brigham Young University; was employed for twenty years as an editor in the Curriculum Department of The Church of Jesus Christ of Latter-day Saints; edited and reported for the *Magna* (Utah) *Times* newspaper for two years; with the former Linda Jean Wells, to whom he was married in 1969, is the father of seven; has resided in Utah since 1971; as literary favorites names Latter-day Saint scripture (including the Bible), Arthur Rimbaud, André Breton, Ezra Pound, T. S. Eliot, Kenneth Rexroth, Gary Snyder, and Philip Lamantia; is the author of *First Light, First Water; Glyphs; Division by Zero;* and *Six Poems by Joseph Smith.*

Acknowledgments

"I sought you, Adonai," *Ensign,* Oct. 1979

"Let the stone whisper to the flower," *Dialogue* 13.4 (1980)

"Like a deer he comes to me," *Dialogue* 13.4 (1980); *Harvest: Contemporary Mormon Poems,* ed. Eugene England and Dennis Clark (Salt Lake City: Signature Books, 1989)

"My beloved shall be mine beyond death," *Ensign,* Feb. 1981

"A daughter of Sarah is my beloved," *Sunstone* 8.6 (1983)

"Adonai: cover me with your robe," *Sunstone* 10.10 (1986); *Harvest* (1989)

"Wedding songs," *Sunstone* 10.10 (1986); *Harvest* (1989)

"Let the grasses sing," *Sunstone* 10.10 (1986)

"Adonai: I have sinned" and "Adonai: forsake me not," *Sunstone* 12.1 (1988)

"Prayer," *Irreantum,* 2006

www.ingramcontent.com/pod-product-compliance
Lightning Source LLC
Chambersburg PA
CBHW022053160426
43198CB00008B/213